the young child

This is an idea book accompanied by clear directions, concise explanations, and a broad range of illustrations and examples. It eliminates the necessity for examining a variety of sources or questioning what principles are best to adopt.

Growing children have been studied from a variety of points of view. **The Young Child: His Activities and Materials** collects and explains practical conclusions regarding every activity of the small child to expand the benefits of play. Much attention is given to story telling, showing how to vary methods to avoid any limitation through sameness, and how to utilize the techniques for purposes beyond entertainment. Play materials are described in this light also. The reader is shown how to make useful toys and how to expand the child's creative art activities in a variety of ways. An abundance of games that children enjoy are described, featuring the learning experiences that can be accomplished through such play. Many of these are games devised by the author for specific purposes. The reader is encouraged not just to use these examples but to create original ones of his own that can be helpful in his training situation.

The book is based on the development patterns of small children and guides the way to improve the regular activities of the growing child. As stated so clearly in the author's foreword:

"The major theme of this book is the creative art activities and play materials which are appropriate for the use of the young child in nursery school and kindergarten. These activities and materials are tied in with the growth pattern of these children. Because play **in Nursery School and Kindergarten** was used extensively throughout the United States and Canada.

`the young child

his activities and materials´

MARGARET A. STANT
Professor Emeritus
University of Maryland

prentice-hall, inc., englewood cliffs, new jersey

ISBN: P 0-13-977157-3

      C 0-13-977165-4

Library of Congress Catalog Card Number: 76-37161

Printed in the United States of America

10 9 8 7 6 5 4 3 2

Prentice-Hall International, Inc., *London*
Prentice-Hall of Australia, Pty. Ltd., *Sydney*
Prentice-Hall of Canada, Ltd., *Toronto*
Prentice-Hall of India Private Limited, *New Delhi*
Prentice-Hall of Japan, Inc., *Tokyo*

This book is humbly dedicated to the thousands of students who have been kind enough to sit through my classes, ask relevant questions, and accept what is hoped has been a creative exposure. These students, undergraduates and graduates, have made my twenty-one years at the University of Maryland a challenging and happy time.

To those who are now teaching in today's exciting new environment of changing education, this book is also dedicated. May these teachers accept and understand what children are trying to say and do when they create with various art media, engage in play, and work with (and in) the many activities of the preschool curriculum.

contents

foreword   xi

acknowledgments   xiii

the young child

1   a thumbnail sketch   1

        PHYSICAL SKETCH, *2*
        INTELLECTUAL SKETCH, *4*
        SOCIAL SKETCH, *6*
        EMOTIONAL SKETCH, *7*
        SUMMARY, *8*

2   his teacher   10

        SEARCH FOR ACTIVITIES, *12*
        SUMMARY, *14*

3   his play and play materials   15

VALUES OF PLAY, *15*
PLAY MATERIALS, *18*
TEACHER-MADE PLAY MATERIALS, *20*
WATERPLAY, *22*
SUMMARY, *25*

4   his pictures   27

STAGES OF GROWTH IN PICTURES, *27*
SEEN IN PICTURES, *31*
SEEKING APPROVAL, *35*
REPEATING PICTURE OR IDEA, *36*
UNFINISHED PICTURES, *36*
SUMMARY, *37*

5   his three-dimensional media   39

BLOCKS, *39*
WORKBENCH, *41*
CLAY, *45*
SANDBOX, *48*
SUMMARY, *48*

6   his other art media   50

PAPER, *50*
PAINTS, *52*
EASELS, *54*
FINGER PAINTING, *55*
STRING PAINTING, *56*
RIBBONS, *57*
TISSUE PAPER AND GLUE, *57*
GADGETS, *58*
CHALK, *58*
COLLAGES, *58*
Q-TIPS, *59*
CRAYONS, *59*
STYROFOAM, *60*
WIRE, *61*
SPATTER PAINTING, *61*
MURALS, *62*
SUMMARY, *63*

7   his music   65

MUSIC APPRECIATION, *65*
RHYTHMS, *66*

DRAMATIZATION, *67*
MUSICAL INSTRUMENTS, *68*
TEACHER-MADE MATERIALS FOR MUSICAL EXPRESSION, *69*
SUMMARY, *70*

8   his puppets   71

USE BY TEACHERS, *71*
CREATING PUPPETS, *73*
PUPPET STAGE, *77*
SUMMARY, *78*

9   his stories   79

BOOK CORNER, *79*
READING BOOKS TO CHILDREN, *80*
VARIATIONS IN PRESENTATION OF STORIES, *81*
TECHNIQUES FOR PRESENTING STORIES, *84*
STORY CONTENT, *85*
SUMMARY, *86*

10   his oral language   87

GREETINGS, *87*
FREE PLAY, *88*
SNACK TIME, *88*
ART, *88*
GAMES, *89*
DRAMATIZATION, *90*
PICTURES AND OBJECTS, *90*
ANIMALS, *91*
TRIPS, *91*
TEACHER OBSERVATIONS, *93*
READING STORIES, *93*
SUMMARY, *93*

11   his science experiences   95

A "DO YOU KNOW" TABLE, *96*
A LIBRARY, *96*
INTERESTS, *97*
ACTIVITIES, *97*
EQUIPMENT, *99*
TEACHER-MADE SCIENCE MATERIALS, *99*
SUMMARY, *105*

12   his mathematics   106

COUNTING, *107*
WORKBENCH, *108*
WATERPLAY, *109*
COOKING, *109*
GARDENING, *109*
BLOCKS, *109*
TRIPS, *110*
SUMMARY, *111*

13   his social studies   112

IN THE SCHOOL, *112*
OUTSIDE THE SCHOOL, *113*
IDEAS FOR SOCIAL ACTIVITIES, *113*
SUMMARY, *115*

14   his games   116

TYPES OF GAMES, *118*
TEACHER-MADE GAMES, *123*
FINGERPLAYS, *125*
SUMMARY, *129*

15   his playground   130

CLIMBING EQUIPMENT, *130*
SANDPILE, *132*
SLIDES, *133*
SWINGS, *133*
OUTDOOR PLAY HOUSE, *134*
OTHER EQUIPMENT, *135*
ADDITIONS TO EXISTING PLAYGROUND EQUIPMENT, *135*
SUMMARY, *136*

16   his creative setting   138

PROPERTY OF CREATOR, *138*
TEACHER INTERFERENCE, *139*
TIME FOR THE CREATOR, *139*
VARIATIONS IN MATERIALS, *139*
WORKING CONDITIONS, *139*
SOMETHING OLD, SOMETHING NEW, *140*
ALONE OR TOGETHER, *140*
SUMMARY, *140*

foreword

This book evolved from the author's teaching a course in activities and materials for many years, during which time a text could not be found which seemed appropriate for the material covered by the course. Through the use of several books, most of the necessary information was located, but it seemed logical to have all information within one textbook.

The major theme of this book is the creative art activities and play materials which are appropriate for the use of the young child in nursery school and kindergarten. These activities and materials are tied in with the growth pattern of these children. Because play materials and art media enter into all facets of the program, other areas of the child's school life are also covered—mathematics, oral language, social studies, science and stories.

The book is intended to serve both as a basic text for college students and as a guide for teachers and administrators who are working in school systems. There is also material which could be used effectively by day care centers and by Headstart groups.

The photographs which appear in the book have been selected from slides which the author has made during the years of in-service work and as a college professor. The black and white drawings are from the author's booklet titled, *Let's Try This in Nursery School and Kindergarten*, which is being incorporated as a part of this book.

The author is indebted to Wendy Eisman of the Bethesda-Chevy Chase Cooperative Nursery School for allowing the use of the Plastic Puppet Heads picture and to the creator of the "Interest Center", Mrs. Joan Welling. A special thanks to Amy Cicchetti for her help in editing this book.

M. A. S.

College Park, Maryland

acknowledgments

The author wishes to express gratitude to the following members of the staff of the College of Education, University of Maryland who offered suggestions and guidance during the writing of this book:

Dr. Robert Ashlock (Mathematics)
Dr. Joan Moyer (Social Studies)
Dr. Glenn Blough (Science)
Mrs. Shirley Shelley (Music)

the young child

1   the young child

a thumbnail sketch

Those who are teaching or who are about to teach the young child of from 2 years of age through 5 years of age will find him at one of the most interesting periods of growths in the lives of children. His outgoing nature —uninhibited conversations, curiosity, and complete frankness—provides the teacher with an understanding of what he needs, thinks, and wishes to do or be.

These children develop at a fast rate during the ages of 2 to 5 years. At each age level there seems to be a special need that requires satisfaction on the part of the child. Although there are variations among children, there are still many characteristics which are common to specific age groups.

The 2-year-old needs a wide expanse of territory to explore, smell, taste, look at, and feel. He investigates anything that comes in contact with his exploring body, as he goes from one thing to another giving each "find" just a few minutes of his time. There is so much to discover when you at last take to the "open road".

When he is 3 years of age the child needs social contacts his own age. He begins reaching out to his peers, even though it may be a nonsocial approach such as a hit or push as he passes a child. There seems to be an instant attraction when a 3-year-old meets another child regardless of the age of the stranger, and without any preliminary advances the child is by the other child's side touching him, or just looking at him.

At 4 years of age the child is at the stage where he needs a pal. The sex of the chum is not important. What is important is that the child now has a friend. This associate becomes a part of all his activities. They seek each other's company, sitting side by side as they eat, work, or play. When resting, their mats are so close together that it looks like one large mat on which the two are reclining. If his pal is the opposite sex he will often declare his intentions of marrying the friend.

When he is 5, the child not only makes social contacts, but becomes interested in group contacts. His play becomes more directive. The children play together, work out ideas together, and often depend on each other's abilities as they recognize them. The child of 5 may become a part of small groups (two to four children or more), and these experiences help him understand his expanding world and also help him understand himself and others. He is beginning to learn that not all people think and behave as he does.

The exploring of the 2s; the social stretching out of the 3s; the pal companion need of the 4s; the group experience needs of the 5s—all these stages need good guidance and help to understand and establish each child's importance and needs, as a separate entity from the group. This is one of the functions of a good nursery school and kindergarten.

Before talking about the activities provided the young child in nursery school and kindergarten, let's take a quick look at what kind of person he is. Only by knowing the child will the teacher know what to give him in the way of learning experiences.

PHYSICAL SKETCH

No one who has ever taught young children will dispute the fact that they are perpetually active, seldom still. They enter work and play with their whole bodies. They feel, smell, observe, and sometimes taste materials and objects. This is their way of learning about things—through the use of their senses.

activity

The child's activity, in all phases of the nursery school and kindergarten programs, may be observed during any part of the school day. He rests and his fingers are making designs on the floor. He pulls at his mat as he rests. He makes rhythmical noises on the floor or table as he works. He listens to a story read by the teacher, and although he is listening his mouth may be be making slight sounds, his fingers may be picking at some part of his body, or his feet may be wiggling. He becomes absorbed in working with art media, but as he concentrates on his production his feet are swinging or tapping in rhythm. He cuts with scissors and he chews his tongue in time to his cutting. His body is a perpetual motor whose switch is seldom turned to "off".

restlessness

Due to his need for physical movement, it is difficult to keep a young child in a sitting or lying position for too long a period of time. If he sits too long his body begins to droop or he begins to wiggle with restlessness. "Let my body move, run, hop, jump, or fly through space!" he seems to say to the teacher.

This restlessness appears in the 2- and 3-year-olds after about five minutes (or less) of quiet participation. The 4-year-olds are capable of taking a little more sitting and may be a captive audience for about ten minutes. The 5-year-olds, with their added maturity, may even be happy through fifteen minutes of sitting or being confined to one position.

The teacher who knows her group's attention span may easily arrange her daily program to include just the right amount of quiet and activity. She must also take into consideration the different attention spans among the same age groups. This year's children may be more restless than last year's and, therefore, can't be expected to have the same span of attention. The one thing the teacher stresses in planning is that the greater part of the day be an active time for these young children.

blinking

Watching a 5-year-old, in particular, the teacher may notice much blinking of eyes as the child works or plays. This is the child's way of resting his eyes, or of focusing a little better on the work at hand. He is a blinker whose eyelids keep in active motion with other parts of his moving body. But the teacher protects the eyesight of these children by watching that sunlight does not shine directly on their work; that the sun is not directly on the book she is reading and showing them; that very tedious close work is not given to these children; that she does not display a picture or something transparent by holding it in front of a window to have children look at it.

largeness

Preschool children admire bigness and strength. Often, when asked to select someone with whom to play, or someone to lead the group, or someone to go on an errand, the children will select the largest child in the group—not because of the child's ability, but because they admire his size.

In turn, these children endeavor to have themselves recognized for their own strength and largeness. "Let me move that piano," a boy will say. He then will push with vigor against the immovable object and after a few grunts and pushes may say, "There. I did it." Tasks beyond his ability are just a way of telling adults and peers that he is to be respected for his supposed strength. In his dramatic play the child takes the part of astronauts, large animals, and other large and outstanding characters to support his feeling of largeness.

imaginary illnesses

At times the child may have imaginary illnesses. His head or stomach may cause him great distress, so much so that he can't go to school. Yet, it may be difficult for him to definitely pinpoint the location of the pain, which he may have in his head and call a stomachache. The pains can be real or make-believe ones, but a pretend pain permits the child to stay at home for a special reason. Something may be going on at home that he doesn't want to miss, or something may be happening at school that he would rather miss.

INTELLECTUAL SKETCH

Today's child has many advantages, such as television, greater access to wide travel, and the advantages of associating to a greater extent with the community around him. These advantages affect him in many ways, one of which is intellectually.

language

The young child has an understanding of many words that could not have been found in the vocabulary of children of fifteen years ago. Not only has he added more and newer words to his vocabulary, but he has also added the meaning of these words in his use of them. Listen to some 5-year-olds talking as they work in the house corner:

> Nancy: I have a fish—three of them and one got hungry and ate the other one. He could only swim down because his tail was gone.
>
> Janet: I have a turtle. He is hibernating. When somebody picks him up he bites. His name is Penny.
>
> Lois: I have a little pet snake. He bit me there (points to finger). He gets angry. That's why he bites you. I was holding him introducing him to my guinea pig.
>
> Mark: You want to know something. Some snakes go 'round scaring people.
>
> Toni: Yeh! Some are so big they can eat you.
>
> Mary: On TV a snake squeezes a man.

future outlook

Teachers working with these children realize that the future is a vague thing as far as these young ones are concerned. They are living in the present and sometimes are unaware of what future time means.

This time concept was made clear to one teacher when a 3-year-old asked her:

> Bruce: Is this tomorrow?
>
> Teacher: Why?
>
> Bruce: Because I go to nursery school on tomorrows.

This misunderstanding on the boy's part was explained later on by his mother. The child would ask her on Sunday if he would be going to school that day. His mother had replied several Sundays, "No, you go to nursery school tomorrow".

imagination

The child's imagination takes him into many strange and wonderful worlds and situations. One child in a kindergarten said good-bye to his teacher each day and always added the following statement: "Good-bye. I have to go now and catch an octopus for my mother's lunch." Another 5-year-old boy drew a picture of a man on a horse and told his peers: "I am the biggest cowboy in the world. Here I am on my horse. And you know what? I just killed George Washington". When the children began arguing with him that Washington had died long ago and therefore he could not have killed him, the boy quickly replied, "Well, anyway, I killed his ghost".

This imagination is found in children's stories, pictures, and dramatic play. The imagination takes the form of aiding the child to enter the world of his own making and allowing him to enact anything he wants through drawing, speaking, or dramatizing.

At times it may be necessary for the teacher to curb some of the child's fantasy by bringing the child back to reality. Imagination can take the child too far away from what is real, if he is continuously living in a make-believe world. One boy tried to escape the reality by telling fantastic tales which always involved himself:

> Bruce: Every night I go for a walk in the woods.
>
> Teacher: How nice! What do you see?
>
> Bruce: I see tigers, and I chase them.
>
> Teacher: Oh!
>
> Bruce: Yes, and sometimes I ride on their backs.
>
> Teacher: You do?
>
> Bruce: And sometimes I pull their tails.
>
> Teacher: You like tigers, don't you?
>
> Bruce: Yeh!
>
> Teacher: So do I. I find them in my woods, too, and I chase them, ride on their backs, and pull their tails.

Bruce (looking rather surprised and after some hesitation): You're making that up, aren't you?

Teacher: Yes. But sometimes it's fun to pretend. But it is also nice to let people know when you are just making believe and when you are telling a true story.

Bruce: I guess we told make-believe ones, huh?

curiosity

Many young children are curious and eager to know about many things. Their questions often place the teacher in a position of wondering how to give an answer or how to look up an answer. "How does a turtle grow from a little one to a big one?"; "How does the snake get out of his skin?"; "What makes the boat float?"; "What is a star made of?"; "Why don't you have a baby?" are a few typical questions offered by one such child. And the questions go on and on.

Answers cannot always be delayed because this child, so curious for an answer to a question on Monday, doesn't remember asking it when the answer is brought to him on Friday. As one child said to his teacher, "Who wants to know?" when she happily told him she had found the answer to his inquiry of five days before.

SOCIAL SKETCH

Young children have certain interests in social living and these interests appear to center around their own family and their peers in the school and neighborhood.

self

The child, however, is concerned mostly about himself and his own activities. What can things do for him? What good are things and what can he do with them? These are questions he wants to have answered about people and things. Everything seems to start with him and, as he reaches out into his environment and comes in contact with people and objects, he makes these new discoveries a part of his life and fits them into his own world. Ask him why he likes someone and his usual reply is, "Because he gets me candy (or some other thing); because he tells me stories; because he takes me places."

me-stage

If the child is 2 or 3 years of age he usually plays alone, learning about play materials and all the wonderful things of the school through working with toys. He even talks to these inanimate objects, but seldom works cooperatively with other children. He may work beside other children without interplay and often without conversation. He is still in the *me-stage*, striving to learn more about himself and his place in the social structure. After he learns about himself, he will be ready to extend his social living and work and play to others.

pals

As the child reaches a more mature level—about 4 years of age—he begins to associate more with the members of the group in play situations. Pals become a part of his life and children play in groups of two and sometimes three. But for the most part, there is a best friend who takes the greater part of the child's time and thoughts. The child is beginning to see the advantage of others helping him, fighting for him, working with him. But ME is still important.

group play

At 5 years of age the child is becoming a more social individual. He may work in groups of four or five children on a project or in dramatic play. Yet, he is still concerned mostly with himself.

seeking approval

Adult approval is a need of these young children, especially at age 5. He uses these requested evaluations from his elders as a means of approving of himself. It may be something he has made which he shows the teacher and asks her if she likes it. It may be a direct question as to whether or not the teacher likes him. It may just be a question such as, "I did it right, didn't I?" Whatever the question, he is asking the adult to approve what he has done or what he is.

EMOTIONAL SKETCH

These children are quick to let their emotions be known. They will not hesitate to tell a peer or an adult exactly how they feel about them. One of the biggest weapons used against their peers is to threaten them with, "You can't come to my birthday party, then." This usually works wonders in getting the verbalizer exactly what he wants. The usual comment directed to the teacher when a child does not get what he wants is, "I'm not coming to this school anymore." This does not work as effectively on the teacher as the child's comments do on his peers.

amenability

Some teachers feel that the young child is almost too docile at times. He obeys well and follows directions as given, especially at 5 years of age. This can be carried to extremes by the teacher, because she can have the children responding to her every demand. She may even get children to sit for long periods of time without any talking. They may not like it, but they comply because the teacher wants it. This is really taking advantage of a child who is so willing to please. He *does* need time to follow his own ideas, to work out some of his own problems, and to think for himself.

anger

A child's anger is displayed in short spurts. He may throw something down in a fit of anger or slam a door because someone has made him mad, but these spurts pass quickly and the next moment the child has forgotten all about his anger. What a lesson the world could take from these children!

personal world

The schoolroom becomes another world to him and the child is sometimes a little reluctant to share his feeling and experience of this new world. His parents may continuously ask him what he has been doing in school. The child may just say he is "doing nothing," or he may say he has "just played."

However, if he is not questioned too much, the child will share this school world with the family when *he* is ready to do so. This is his first opportunity to have an experience of his own, outside the home. It becomes his haven of refuge, his own private world.

Many children, whose parents expect a picture or some other product each day when the child returns home, will usually get it. But the parent should see the child's lack of interest, and slight effort, as he produces the required object. Maybe five minutes before he leaves the schoolroom he will take a piece of paper and scribble something on it. This is for mother who is waiting at home with outstretched hand to receive the child's output for the day!

SUMMARY

With what kind of child are teachers dealing in nursery school and kindergarten? It may be summed up in the following statement by a 5-year-old girl:

> Adult: Who do you think is the smartest person in the world?
>
> Child: That's a hard question, but I guess I am the smartest.

This answer by the child might cause various responses from adults. Some might say, "He's cute"; "He's sure of himself"; "He's been bragged about too much"; "He thinks a lot about himself"; "He has the whole world revolving around himself." All these responses would fit into the picture of what young children are like.

Of course, he does cute things. Everyone would admit that.

Of course, he feels sure and independent. Independence has been a goal set by the family and teachers.

Of course, he is self-centered and brags about himself. He is still searching for his place in the world and working out his relationships with people and things.

Of course, the world revolves around him. From infancy his needs have been satisfied by everybody and everything in his immediate environment. It takes time to learn that someone else is just as important, or knows more, or is prettier, or can make something better.

So, as teachers work with the young child they need to apply the findings of child development. What is known about this child is important in planning a program for him. This program is based on what is known about children at particular stages of growth. Blending this knowledge with the teacher's understanding of the democratic process, she can give meaning to a program for the young child.

Maybe the teacher's slogan could be, "Let me not teach these children too fast for they are living in their present world, not in an adult's present world or a child's future world."

2   the young child

his teacher

How far can, or should, nursery school and kindergarten teachers go in advancing the program for young children? Should they wait to see if the children need more than they are being exposed to in the everyday experiences provided in the classroom? Should they provide extra stimulation to test the group's capabilities and potentials? Should they base additions to the program mainly on the interests of the children? Should they add new materials and equipment on the basis of the interests and maturity of the group?

Teachers often feel the need to stimulate or challenge children beyond the usual provisions of the curriculum. This need stems from a variety of causes.

Some teachers follow a prescribed curriculum in which mental stimulation is stressed. Others find themselves bored with the same program year after year. Some teachers find that children are asking for more than they are receiving from a school's program. Some teachers feel that it is important to stimulate a group to learn the usual as well as the unusual. Some teachers believe that children are not challenged sufficiently by programs based entirely on children's interests. Some feel that the nursery school and kindergarten programs need a *new face* to keep both children and teachers interested.

In the background are current pressures from parents, educators, and laymen who think children are capable of taking on much more than they are being given. Many programs in education are being evaluated in terms of any or all of these pressures.

Today's market is flooded with gadgets, programs, techniques, and corrective devices, most of which claim to be a cure-all for the ills of education. These ills vary in degree and kind in accordance with the position of the writer. Many of the ideas advanced come from people who have never taught in a classroom. These people base their ideas on what education should be, in contrast or in accordance with the education they received. In some cases the instigator of the new idea could have had a good or bad experience in his school situation and is asking that children have as good as he had, or better than he had. Do they always take into consideration the changing times, which call for changes in education to fit a new and different world?

Probably the most important indication that a teacher should add to, extend, or change the program of her classroom is the interest or needs shown by the children in particular subjects or areas. The children's questions and explorations often alert the teacher. Perhaps the children are searching for information, are trying to solve a problem, or are simply curious. Their interest is an important signal for teachers for it can point to significant needs of the individual or the group.

The teacher constantly should ask herself, "Just what is the child ready for?" Only by repeated testing and trying can she find the answer. At times she presents a stimulus which yields no response on the part of the children. So, she must try something else. The cycle of trial and error is an endless one in any teaching-learning process.

Although interest signals on the part of the children are important, the teacher cannot always wait for spontaneous interest to stimulate learning. She might wait all year to find that little happens. Frequently she will find a need to present advanced ideas, equipment, and supplies. These will foster an interest or curiosity in something the children have not yet experienced. Always the teacher must remember the maturity level of her group, and the individual differences within that group. She must note the enthusiasm with which new ideas or materials are accepted by the children. She must recognize the implications that variations in the program will have for the group and for the total program.

An example of an enthusiastic reception of new ideas occurred one day in a nursery school group. Joe came to school and hurriedly sought out his teacher. "Guess what?" he asked the teacher as soon as he walked through the door. "We have termites in our house!" The two chatted for a while about this occurrence, but the teacher noticed that this experience did not cease with this one conversation. Joe talked enthusiastically throughout the morning with any child with whom he came in contact. He explained to each what an exciting thing was going on at his house. "I can't see them but they leave holes," he told the children.

The teacher thought she might carry this interest a little further as there had seemed to be acceptance on the part of the other children in sharing in Joe's experience. She spent a good part of that night drawing pictures of termites. She made them large enough for children to see their shape and their activity in wood.

The next day she showed these drawings to the group after the story hour. Joe added further details about where these insects were in his house. He added the fact that they were also in his outdoor lamp post.

Most of the children added to the discussion and the teacher, elated with her success, decided to continue this phase of the program. For two days she brought in more drawings, first of butterflies and then of beetles. The children appeared interested.

On the third day she brought in another idea and showed the children the pictures she had drawn of ants and their activities. Joe, sitting in the back of the group, leaned over to George and exclaimed, "Mrs. G. really likes bugs, doesn't she?" Yes, teachers can go too far in bringing in the unusual or the unknown, or in following the interests of children.

Books can help the teacher in selecting materials and ideas for her classroom, but the best guide for her to follow is herself. *She* knows the children, their backgrounds, their interests and needs. Therefore, she is governed by her own observations, ideas, and judgments. She should have an awareness of materials in order to stimulate an exciting program.

SEARCH FOR ACTIVITIES

The teacher is always searching for activities that are applicable in the nursery school and kindergarten classroom. Some of the ideas presented here may stimulate the thinking of teachers who say, "That idea is good, but I would do it this way; so I'll change this." She would use *her* ideas to fit her way of teaching, her children's understandings and needs, her type of program. Everyone needs to teach the way she feels and enjoys. A real teacher approves of what she is doing, and is happy and content with the young children.

Teachers often ask, "What should I give children in the way of productive activities?" "What are children ready for at age 4?" "What can I present to 5-year-olds that will be challenging and beneficial?" The answers might be, "What kind of children are you teaching? What is the children's background of experiences? What are the children's needs and interests? What materials and facilities does the school afford?"

If the teacher's aim is materials that provide large muscle development, then she must have the equipment that encourages the use of these muscles. She can't provide for a child's social adjustments unless he has things to see, people to talk to, and peers to work with. She can't provide a chance for the child to express ideas (original or otherwise) if the child is not given opportunities to talk, talk, talk, and try, try, try. She can't provide for creativity if a child is not given time, space, materials, and experiences to permit him to express himself in proper surroundings, with the proper guidance.

When a teacher wants to give children materials to use in a creative manner, her first look is at the school facilities, the children's acquired knowledge, and the materials which can be used and manipulated by children of this mental age, plus the teacher's knowledge of child development, and the expectations of children at various developmental levels.

Who thought twenty years ago, that children of 5 and sometimes 3 and 4 years of age would be discussing space travel? Who knows what their interests may be in the near future with our changing world? It has been necessary to change our language, our play materials, and our books to coordinate with our modern world. Children are very aware of the many changes going on in their lives. Is the teacher also alert to these innovations?

Take the case of the 3-year-old boy who was in nursery school the day a spaceship carried an astronaut into space. The child's feelings about this event were directed to the teacher in his language:

> Child: Teacher, there's a man up there (points to sky).
>
> Teacher: There is?
>
> Child: And you know what? He's all wrapped up in metal so he won't get hurt.
>
> Teacher: I'm glad he's safe.
>
> Child: And you know what? He's flying all around our nursery school.
>
> Teacher: Would you like to listen to the radio and hear what the man is doing?
>
> Child: Oh, boy! Then I can hear him come back home!

Working with the needs of today's children leads the teacher to center her curriculum around the wonderful occurrences, the thrills of today's world, the things that are America, and the fast-moving pace of today's living.

teacher's role

Stimulated and encouraged by the teacher, the child approaches the creative life of his school in his own unique manner. This stimulation and encouragement offered by the teacher can be presented in a variety of ways.

Time. By allowing the child to finish work once he has begun something, the teacher is admitting that the creative urge cannot be stopped by signals, especially when the child is consumed with interest and a desire to finish. The teacher must consider if the reading of a story or a science session is more important for the child than the finishing of an absorbing idea.

Materials. Adding new or suggestive materials in a conspicuous place in the room may inspire the children to use these supplies in the creation of their work. Bits of paper napkins, sheets of cleaning tissue, bits of cotton, or pieces of netting are suggestive things which children might decide to use as clouds in a picture. A child may use small pieces of twigs for fences or tracks or the trunks of small trees.

Criticism. By avoiding evaluation and criticism of the children's work, there is less possibility of the teacher dampening the children's creativity. Do horses have to have four legs showing? (Maybe the legs are not seen because the horse is standing with his farther legs hidden behind his depicted legs.) Maybe this *is* a tailless cat! Maybe the house doesn't have windows on the side shown in the picture!

Experiences. By giving the child experiences, both in and out of the class-room, the teacher and parents widen the child's horizons. Subsequently, his ideas may be clarified or strengthened. One day in University of Maryland Laboratory School, a basketball basket was placed on the side of the playground building. Children were drawn to it immediately. The teacher heard a boy say, "Look, we're going to play football," as he picked up the ball and threw it toward the basket.

The teacher, without any comments, took the children on a trip the next day to watch football players practicing. Hearing the word "football" and seeing players in action relayed to the children what the word "football" meant. "We don't play football at nursery school, do we?" one of the boys asked the teacher. "No," answered the teacher, "but we do play basket-ball, don't we?"

Assistance. By watching and noting when help is needed, the teacher can step in and offer help to the child. She must remember, as this assistance is given, that what the child is making is *his*—his art effort, his personal interpretation. So, she must beware of overassistance. She does not place any marks or additions on the child's work. She places his name on the back of the paper in the upper left hand corner. This acquaints the child with the left-to-right movement of writing. It also gives him opportunity to observe the writing of letters, and the fact that writing begins at the top of the paper and continues in a downward direction.

Another "no" for teachers: Remember not to cut children's pictures into different shapes after the child completes his work. If his production is cut into Easter egg shapes, Christmas tree shapes, or any other form which is to be used as room decoration, the teacher is destroying the child's creation.

SUMMARY

Teachers must be forever on the alert to satisfy the needs and interests of the children. At the same time, they must remember to challenge them to further learnings by introducing the *unknown* into the program. This makes children aware of the world around them and the possibilities of keeping eyes and ears open for new findings, new discoveries. To fulfill this responsibility is a challenge—to do it well makes teaching worthwhile.

3   the young child

his play and play materials

Play materials in the nursery school and kindergarten offer the young child a variety of advantages. Play helps a young child learn about himself, about others, and about the world around him. The child organizes this play, he cooperates with other children in their play, and learning occurs. But what does he learn?

VALUES OF PLAY

If one watches a young child at play, growth and learning within the child become apparent. He may enter the group as a child who plays alone, and leave the group a leader. He may enter the group as a nonsocial individual, and become a socially accepted member of his class. Let's look at some of the things which bring about changes in the child and, at the same time, add to his learning as he plays alone and with others.

a child grows up

Adults often refer to the young child as small. They may say to him, "You are not big enough to reach that"; "You can do that when you are older"; or "That's too heavy for you to carry. You are too little."

So the child becomes more aware of his smallness, because of the unthinking remarks of the adult in his everyday life. Watch the child's face when he is told, "How big you are"; "It's good to have such a strong boy around."

The child may (if only for a short time) enter into a world where he can accomplish those things which his smallness prevents him from doing through the use of men's ties, hats, briefcases, vests, shoes, ladies' dresses (shortened), ribbons, scarves, hats, shoes, and pocketbooks. He puts on a vest and picks up a briefcase, and suddenly he is transformed into a *daddy* going to work. A girl dons a woman's dress, drapes a lace scarf over her head, and she is a *bride.* In these assumed roles, no one can tell the children they are too small to be going to work or too little to be a bride.

a child reaches understandings

How does it feel to wash dishes as mothers do? How does it feel to telephone as parents do? How does it feel to make decisions about meals, bedtime, clothing, going places?

A child tries to gain these understandings, and others, by dramatizing with materials available to him in nursery school and kindergarten. In this way he may also work out some misunderstanding, or solve some problem, which has been bothering him. "What shall we have for breakfast?" asks the child taking the part of the mother. "Let's have chocolate cake", replies the "father." This decision in real life would be fun!

a child plays roles

Through play, the child may make himself anything he wishes. He can be an animal, any object, any adult, any other child. His imagination can be used to change him quickly from a lion to a baseball player, and then to a snake. This is his way of learning about things and people. It may even help him overcome some fear he has as he enacts the antics and noises of animals, snakes, and people.

a child relives situations

Many times the child will recall an experience (and not always right after he has had the experience, but maybe weeks later) by placing himself in a situation in which he acts out what he has seen and heard. This is his way of clarifying what he has witnessed and, at the same time, strengthening his concepts and observations.

a child releases emotions

Play offers the young child times to express anger, dislike, disagreement, and insecurity in a play situation. Materials, such as dolls, clay, punching bags (cloth ones stuffed with styrofoam or newspaper), and boxing gloves, permit the child to act out his feelings through play in a constructive manner.

a child learns concepts

Play materials give the child an understanding of size, shape, and color. A puzzle aids him in seeing likenesses of shapes as he selects puzzle pieces to fit into the right places. He notes as he plays with the dishes that certain sizes fit together. He matches colors using peg boards and colored blocks. He matches dresses according to the size of the doll, and realizes that some are too small, some too large, and some just right.

a child expresses interests

Much children's play is based on what they like the most and what they are interested in. A boy may prefer play materials that offer an opportunity to construct, to operate. He may use materials which require large muscle manipulation. Girls may be more inclined to use quieter materials—dolls, puzzles, or materials related to family living. This does not mean that boys do not like family activities or that girls do not like large motor toys.

a child can play alone

There is a need for all people to be alone at some time. The child is no exception to this. Therefore, some toys are on hand to supply the child with a chance for individual play. Many other toys are there when he needs cooperative play. It is necessary to have some of each type in a preschool group. One child expressed his joy in being alone when the teacher asked the 4-year-old if he would like to have another child join him, as he worked in the house corner. The child's reply answered her question with exact meaning being expressed. "Teacher," he said with his hands on his hips and his head tilted to one side, "don't you know there are times when a guy wants to be alone?"

a child blends into a social world

The child shares the world of his peers through his play. At the same time, he shares *his* world with the other members of his school group. The children absorb from each other, and are often corrected by each other. Listen!

> Marvin: Hey, pass me the Quackers!
>
> Della: Teacher, did you hear what he said? He called Kackers, Quackers.

Or, one may hear corrections of this kind:

> John: That's not how a lion walks. Look!
>
> Mary: It is so.

John: It is not. I'll show you. (He demonstrates.)

Mary: That's not right.

John: It is, too. I saw a lion at the zoo, and he walked like this.

Or, a girl may say to her classmate, "This is the way you put on a diaper. I know, because I saw my mama do it."

Not only is there an intellectual sharing, but also a cooperative sharing of interests. Jim says to Helen, "You get some of those animals, and I'll get some boxes, and boy, we'll make somethin'."

PLAY MATERIALS

Play materials are a vital part of the nursery school and kindergarten child's life. Through the use of these materials he learns about himself, about his peers, about his adult associates, and about his environment.

The materials offer the child a chance to relive what he has experienced or to relive an event, which helps him understand what he has seen and heard. The words "play materials" could be changed to "work materials" because these are the tools of learning that aid the child emotionally, physically, intellectually, and socially. They are his "key" to the door of learning.

There are many types of toys on the market today. It is up to the teacher to know the interests, abilities, and backgrounds of her children, so that she will be able to select toys accordingly.

criteria for selection of play materials

Certain things should be kept in mind as the teacher examines playthings for the children in her classroom. She must be sure the toys are going to serve a purpose, and not just be cute things for the room decoration.

Quantity. If sharing is an important learning experience for these children, then in purchasing materials it is a good idea not to have one of everything for every child. If there are twenty children, maybe eight balls would be enough. This would give children an opportunity to play cooperatively, and take turns using the balls.

However, the younger the children, the lower the ratio between material and child. The youngest age group is not as capable of sharing as they will be at 4 and 5 years of age. This is due to the developmental pattern of the 2- and 3-year-olds who are just beginning to learn about "me." They will be better sharers, after they have found out where and what they are in their environment.

Group Needs. A look at the interests and abilities of her group of children will aid the teacher in selecting materials that add to these interests and abilities. For example, the number of pieces in a puzzle would depend on the ability of the children. Are they ready for three pieces, ten pieces, twenty pieces? It is often a good idea to start with a simple puzzle and progress to a more complicated one as the children master each puzzle.

Durability.   More and more schools are spending money on a smaller amount of toys, but selecting toys that will endure through the years. Hardwood play materials are being preferred to the fragile plastic toys that were once bought in large quantities only to have wheels break off trucks, arms off dolls, and handles off shovels after a few usings. Sometimes, it was a child who stepped on a plastic toy that had been left on the floor, and it was crushed underfoot.

Multipurpose Activities.   Many modern toys, rather than looking exactly like a specific object, are now appearing in "unstructured form." The wood is carved to suggest a person, but it could be any age, sex, or color. It becomes what the child wants it to be. The child is called upon to use his imagination, and to suit the toy to the dramatization or play in which he is involved.

Safety.   Toys as nearly safe as possible are the best to buy. Teachers watch for roughness in material, for sharp edges, and for toxic paint. It is always wise to read the label before buying play materials. They should be labeled "nontoxic" or "lead-free" if they are painted, or should have some other designation as to their safety if placed in young mouths.

ideas for extra toys

Certain inexpensive materials may be added to the house corner to increase the dramatic play and satisfy the needs of some of the children.

Alarm Clock Or Wall Clock.   Clocks are good for exploration by children. What fun it is to be able to take something apart and, at the same time, learn something about the object.

An alarm clock gives children the possibility of examining and learning, if the teacher can find an old clock which is no longer useful. If the numbers are large and clear, the children will have contact with mathematics. The clock can be set and used as a warning for a "stopping time," a "get ready time," or a "pick-up time."

After the children have tired of using the clock as a toy, the teacher may add further interest for the group by removing the back of the clock, and exposing the works. When the children start taking the clock apart, supervision becomes necessary because of the sharp springs that the teacher would have to remove.

Sewing Baskets.   This could also be a contribution to the house corner. The teacher could place a covered basket, or cardboard box, in the housekeeping portion of the room. Inside the basket or box, she could place large needles, heavy thread, pieces of material, buttons, and a pair of blunt scissors. Ribbons, tape, and bows may also be added.

Material of this type is for the children who *want* to sew—maybe to repair a doll's dress. Sewing is not encouraged because it is difficult for the very young child to attempt. His eyes may not be ready for this type of close work, or his skill in handling needle and thread may not be developed. The sewing basket is merely a house addition which is used when children feel the need for its use. Some schools use yarn sewing needles (plastic), and have pieces of burlap for sewing material.

ideas for extra play activities

Current Events. When children show an interest in some current happening, extend and sponsor this interest with interesting props. Goggles, cylindrical blocks, helmets, round cardboard cans, and earphones may add to the dramatic play of space travel.

If it is a circus that is creating an interest, the teacher may add large pieces of cotton (for fur), ribbons and ropes (for tightrope walkers), large boxes (for cages), scarves (for aerialists), wooden horses (for riders), and any other materials which would add to the children's dramatization of circus activities.

Puzzles. Use the children's pictures to make some extra puzzles for the classroom. When a child decides which of his pictures he would like to have used for a puzzle, the teacher can mount the picture on thin cardboard. Then, the picture is cut into large pieces—the number of pieces depending upon the ability of the group. (Be sure each piece has an identifying shape or color.) Children enjoy trying one another's puzzles.

TEACHER-MADE PLAY MATERIALS

There are various easy-to-make materials which may be created by a teacher for use by the children. Construction and content of the materials will depend on the teacher's objectives. In order to meet one or more objectives, some materials may require an addition or subtraction from the ideas presented in the bought item.

Things that might not be found in a store, and would not cost very much to make are sometimes fun to try and a pleasure to create. The main thing is to make them sturdy so that rough handling will not destroy them in a few uses.

materials for dramatic play

Teachers are very often called collectors of everything. The word "junk" is often applied to their hoard of materials being saved for a time when they may be useful. The so-called junk becomes useable, lovely materials for children as the teacher applies her skill in making play activity toys. Here are some ideas for materials for children to use in their dramatic play.

Clock. The top of a large potato chip can can easily become the face of a clock. And what fun the children will have moving the hands and setting the clock!

After painting the top of the can, apply ready-made numbers which may be purchased in art stores. If the teacher does not require such artistic numbers, then she may make the numbers from thick cardboard, plastic, or felt. For clock hands the teacher could use any heavy material (wood, plastic, metal), and attach them to the center of the clock face.

Paint one side of the clock red and one side blue to indicate that red is *after* the hour and blue is *before* the hour in order to help children tell time using the minutes of the clock.

Be sure the small hand is touching the numbers as it turns, and that the large hand extends slightly beyond all the numbers. Young children, with their spatial difficulties, sometimes need to have things designated by objects touching, or by children's hands touching, the thing or number.

Beauty Parlor Or Barber Shop.   Many small girls and boys enjoy playing beauty parlor and barber shop. This is just another of their grown-up plays which can be aided by the use of props. A teacher may make a play "dryer" by attaching a sturdy round hat box to an L-shaped wooden frame (or an old-fashioned lamp stand). Add some curlers, pillow cases with holes cut for sliding over heads, and a make-believe shaver. Children use this material at a table on which a mirror has been placed.

Paper Foods.   These are easily made and are life-size and, therefore, more realistic. Using a wad of newspaper, apply strips of newspapers by using liquid starch to help the strips stick to the wad. As paper is applied the mass will become malleable, and can be shaped as layers of paper are applied. Make bananas, oranges, apples, steaks, loaves of bread, and any other foods children can use to play house in the schoolroom.

Paper Dishes.   Paper stripping may also be used to create large dishes for use in the doll corner. The creating of such material would depend on the teacher's feelings about what size dishes would be appropriate for use by the children. Is it better for children to use large dishes in the house corner, so their dramatization will be more realistic and less like playing with doll dishes? If so, create salad size dishes to hold a variety of make-believe food.

Take a salad dish and grease the bottom of the plate with a thin coating of white vaseline. Take narrow strips of newsprint, dip them in water, and apply them to the bottom of the greased dish.

When the dish bottom is completely covered, start dipping strips of newspaper in a mixture of liquid starch and water (about two-thirds starch and one-third water). Apply about four or five coats of paper strips to the dish bottom; then cover with strips of toweling or plain newsprint, again using the starch mixture and set aside to dry. After drying, the paper form may be easily removed from the plate to be painted and decorated as desired.

Birthday Cake.   Start with a large tin cake box or cookie tin. Place narrow paper strips made from newspaper over the entire tin until it is covered with about three layers of paper. The paper strips are dipped first into the starch and water mixture described above. Criss-cross these strips over the box rather than placing them all in the same direction.

When dry, this "cake" may be iced by using Ivory Snow mixed with water to a thick consistency. Spread the icing on the cake and while it is still wet, place candle holders in the icing.

materials for self-help

By using certain kinds of toys a child may learn to perform an everyday task. In a play way the task becomes less tedious, and the child may apply what he has learned on the material to what is required of him in his real world.

Gadget Apron.   Cut out an apron which will fit the children. Do this on a double fold of material so that the shoulder seams are joined after cutting. This will slip easily over children's heads.

On the front of the apron sew a zipper, a button and buttonhole, and a belt with large snaps. On the back of the apron sew a belt with a large buckle, a large hook and eye, and a lacing area.

Children can use this piece of play material while the apron is on their bodies, turning back to front after working on one side. In this way they are working and hopefully mastering some of the everyday tasks they encounter in dressing. *And* they are doing them in the same position required in dressing—not using gadgets in a book or on a shoe.

(Suggestion: When placing the lacing area on the apron, start the lacing from the bottom and work upwards. Use two colors of bright laces and sew them together. Children may then use the colors as guides and may better understand that the yellow goes over the red, rather than remembering that the same color string goes over and under.)

Gadget Board.   When making a gadget board of locks, place each type of lock on a small door that opens when the lock is released. The board is made with depth so that objects may be placed inside the doors for the children to discover. This is one way of introducing new material to the classroom, or it may be used for children to place their contributions for the class to discover.

Lacing Shoe.   Use a discarded man's shoe. Nail it to a large board that can be lifted by the children. Polish the shoe, and lace it with two different colored laces by tying the laces together in the center. The colors help the children remember which color to place on top of the other as they are lacing. This shoe can be placed on the floor in front of the child with the back of the shoe towards his body. Then the child gets a real understanding of how to lace a shoe when it is on him.

WATERPLAY

"Water in my classroom? No, indeed! It's too messy," say some preschool teachers. "Besides," they add, "it is just something for children to play in and they can't do anything with it."

"Oh, but there are real values in waterplay," answer the small minority of teachers who have this play material as a part of the activities in their classrooms. It is these people who are answering the sensory exploratory needs of children.

To understand how and why children gravitate to water, watch an adult playing in the surf, sitting on the beach and splashing the water as it comes to him, or taking a leisurely bath. As he reclines in the bathtub with his head propped on a rubber pillow, he is reading a book. Are these adults getting nothing from this experience?

Water is one of the first sensory experiences a child has. It begins in his infant bath as he splashes the water, flays his arms up, down, and around as the water flies. He is placed on his stomach in the water and he becomes a swimmer, with legs going up, down, in, and out. This is his introduction to a play material which is not resistant to his touch, that can be pushed, splashed, poured, thrown, and dripped. At the same time, it envelops him in a pleasing atmosphere of soothing, cooling, or warming contentment. He is master of this water which is not going to topple over, not going to be used up, or not going to be taken away by one of his peers. This satisfaction makes the waterplay all the more interesting and appealing.

This love for waterplay is brought to nursery school by the 2- and 3-year-olds. He goes to the bathroom, presumably to use the toilet facilities. But his first stop is usually at the sink, where he washes his hands for as long a time as he is permitted to do so. He lets the water run through his hands, over his hands, and tries to catch the stream and hold it in his grasp. It is saying to him, "You do not have to make anything with me. Just enjoy the comfort, the feeling of mastery, the pleasure I can give you through experimenting with me!"

The 4- and 5-year-olds are equally attracted by water. They scrub floors with a toy mop—not always to make it clean, but to have the experience of seeing the water change the color of the floor; to have the experience of seeing water disappear through evaporation; to experience the big muscle development which is required to push the mop.

Perhaps the 5-year-old is asked to wash a table which has been used for snack-time. This is a procedure which sometimes takes ten minutes, although only a few crumbs are on the table. The sponge is dipped in water and rubbed vigorously over the table top. Occasionally the sponge, crumbs, and all is squeezed over the table top to make more residue to be picked up again by the sponge. Even a child in elementary school will beg to stay after school to wash the blackboards.

Many children in nursery school and kindergarten play in water in various ways as a daily practice. Maybe they are prevented from doing this activity at home, and the need for exploring and contacting this medium is answered through the preschool program.

values of waterplay

Other than satisfaction and enjoyment, and the feeling of mastery over material, what other benefits can a child derive from working in and with water? (See also chapter 12, p. 109.)

Solids vs. Liquids.   The teacher has the children mix paints. During this process the child sees a solid (powdered paint) change into a liquid as water is added. The child mixes clay and, again, a solid becomes a semi-solid as water is added to the powdered clay. He mixes salt and flour with water containing vegetable coloring as he makes the dough, and again he sees this same change in material. Through these experiences he begins to see that materials can be changed and sometimes returned to their original state of solidity or fluidity.

Buoyancy.   The teacher places various objects near a pail of water, or near the watertable. She has purposely picked some things that will float and some that will not. By testing these objects the child discovers that water can help some things stay on the surface of the liquid, and that other objects go directly to the bottom. So, science is introduced. This information can be applied later in the child's learnings as he becomes involved in the elementary school science program.

The teacher may introduce these floating and nonfloating materials to the children by first dropping one into the water and seeing what happens. Then she can ask each child to try some object and see what happens. The objects can then be placed in piles according to their reaction after being placed in the water.

Plants and Animals.   Flowers and plants need watering, and a child is always willing to do this chore. He is learning that plants will not grow without one of their basic requirements—water. More science is introduced.

The teacher may place some plants in the room and some in a dark closet and have the children water only the room plants, ignoring those in the closet. Let the children tell what has happened to the two plants.

Children enjoy caring for animals by cleaning out cages with a damp sponge, and giving the animal fresh water. Again, he is learning that animals, like humans, need water and that it must be clean and fresh.

Housekeeping.   Dishwashing and the washing of doll clothes are favorite activities of many children. First of all they are enacting the roles of the adult—they *are* mother washing clothes and dishes. This is helping them understand the activities and roles of their parents.

Children are also witnessing the dissolving of soap as it mixes with the water, and the resulting air bubbles which form as the water is stirred. And, when dishes become too much for one child, the socializing process begins. It may require someone to dry the dishes or someone to put away the clean dishes. Cooperative play develops.

Water Painting.   Pails of water and large brushes are used in some schools to give children an opportunity to paint the playground fence, the steps, or the equipment. The participants are ardent workers—painting and watching the water disappear as the sun absorbs the moisture. Evaporation is being witnessed while the child enjoys making the equipment and fence look like new.

pools

A very few schools have pools in the floor of the classroom which can be covered when not in use, the cover becoming a part of the flooring when the pool is closed. The pool is used for wading, blowing bubbles, floating objects, and using strainers, dippers, plastic containers, and other toys for play and dramatization.

blowing bubbles

Blowing bubbles is interesting play for the young child. He learns that air will form the water into bubbles; that the bubbles will break when the air is released; that you blow out, not in, when you form bubbles. Many other facts are learned as he works with the soapy water.

Bubble pipes may require too much effort on the part of the teachers because of the need for sterilizing the pipes after each using. So teachers often prefer plastic straws or dandelion stems. The latter are cut in a cross at one end, and then flattened, before dipping into the water and blowing.

outdoor fun

Use a water table or tub set either in a grassy or stony part of the yard, so that excess water is drained into the ground. As a holder for the items to be used in the water, use a large piece of pegboard and attach boards to the back so it will stand.

Place round elastic or hooks in the holes of the board and place the dipper, bucket, cup, plastic glass, and other water equipment on this board. This will not crowd the water so much because the floating, measuring, and dipping materials can be taken down as needed and placed back on the board after use. If shapes of objects are outlined on the board, children can match likenesses of shapes and return objects to proper places.

Some days add vegetable dye to the water and give it a lively color. Or add soap suds and create bubbles.

SUMMARY

"But he just plays in nursery school," says the skeptic. Yes, the child plays, but through this play he is working out his understandings of people, situations, and experiences.

As he plays, he overcomes or understands the fears which he has encountered in his short life. He becomes an ape and tries to eat everyone, and his fear of the ape he has seen on TV bcomes less. He pretends to be the make-believe creatures he sees and hears about, and his fears are alleviated.

A teacher most remember in purchasing materials that she must provide for the immature child, as well as the highly intelligent child; that she must provide for toys for individuals, as well as toys for cooperative play; that she must select toys, not for their cuteness or their adult appeal, but for their aesthetic appeal. Do they say to children, "Pick me up. Try me. Discover what I can do. Make something with me," or do they just seem to say, "Admire me."

The teacher who does not have a great amount of money to spend on toys can, in many instances, make her own play equipment which, she hopes, will add to the stimulation of play and learning.

If waterplay can be of value to the child, then the teacher must give him opportunities to test the possibilities of this medium. If no watertable is available, a plastic bathing pool makes a good substitute. This is easy to store, does not take up necessary floor space, and, of course, is cheaper than a table.

If anyone doubts the natural attraction of water for children, follow a child from home to school, or into his own backyard. He sees puddles of water left by the rain or the hose, and steps, stamps, and even plays in them with his hands. To restrain him from this experience would be as difficult as asking him to forget there is chocolate candy on the living room table.

One thing, however, must be kept in mind. There is a difference in using water in a constructive, learning manner and using it to throw at someone, to push someone into, or to splash all over the classroom. Water, like all materials, has its limits and rules in a social setting.

4   the young child

his pictures

The teacher working with a 2- to 5-year-old will undoubtedly find him fascinating, charming, loveable, and full of imagination and inquiry. At no other age will his imagination be used so freely and productively in language arts, dramatic play, musical interpretations, and art media. His uninhibited nature is a joy to the nursery school or kindergarten teacher, and probably a disturbing or puzzling factor to some parents. Mothers and fathers often ask, "Why, why, why does he pretend so much? Why does he make such 'messy' pictures that have no resemblance to anything?"

Taking a look at some of his art work helps adults understand how the child's development and age affect the end product. Stages of growth are noticeable in the pictures he makes, and they help the teacher guide the child in learning, concepts, and art media.

STAGES OF GROWTH IN PICTURES

testing period

Not all small children go through the same stages in their approach to being creative. Whether it is telling stories, dramatizing, doing rhythmic interpretations, painting a picture, working with clay, or building with blocks, the preschool child usually first approaches materials and activities with an experimental or trying out period.

The child picks up a paint brush and makes lines or blots on the paper. Or he covers the paper with a spot of red, over which he applies a spot of green, then a spot of yellow, until his picture resembles a large sea of brown or black paint. He is testing the brush, his control of the brush, and the results he gets when paints are mixed. At the same time, he is testing himself.

One little boy, after using color on color on color, looked at his large sheet of brown paint. He laughingly said, "Look, I just made all the chocolate cake in the world and it's mine."

Sometimes he tests the durability of the paper by scrubbing with his brush until a hole appears in the paper. He may also be testing the brush or the paint. Regardless of his reason for this scrubbing action, he goes about this exploration with feeling and vigor. His face may hold the look of an artist at work as his eyes appraise, his fingers touch, or his voice compliments the painting. The paint may be running down the paper, but his dedication to his job causes him to disregard this fact. He is in the *searching or testing stage.*

There are many varieties of testing that vary with different children. In some cases the child explores by placing the bristles, filled with paint, on the paper and then pushing the brush bristles with his other hand. The result is an interesting lengthwise brush head (Figure 4–1). This is also a sensory experience because hands are in paint as often as they are on the brush handle. The child enjoys the feel of the slippery liquid.

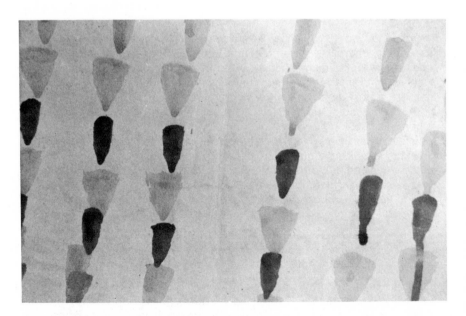

FIGURE 4–1   Result of Using a Brush Head as a Gadget Painter

discovery period

Gradually, as the child gains control of the brush and learns that various strokes make different kinds of designs on the paper, he begins to see pictures in what he has made. "Oh, look," he exclaims with pride and often surprise, "I made a dog." *He* is the only one who knows it is a dog, and he may be the only one who can make out the object in the sea of paint. Yet the teacher begins to realize that the child is now searching for a symbol to express his feelings. Once this symbol is found, and proves satisfactory to him, it will be found in many of his paintings, crayoning, and clay work. This is the *discovery stage.*

predicting period

Next the child begins to paint with a purpose in mind. Before he starts to work he may tell anyone who is within listening distance, "I am going to make a picture of me and my mother." The resulting masterpiece is probably not recognizable to anyone but the creator; but he has reached the stage in producing with media where he has an idea in mind before starting to work. His aim is set before the picture begins (Figure 4–2). He has arrived at what might be called the *predicting stage.*

FIGURE 4–2
A Twin Draws Himself
and his Brother

FIGURE 4–3
Painting of an
Experience Showing
Necessary Details

recognizable period

As the child begins to be more observant of what is around him, his drawings become more detailed. But only those details that are important to the child or that are needed to explain the action are added.

For example, the child draws or paints a rabbit with head, body, and ears. Facial expression and other details are not needed because the ears indicate that *this is a rabbit.* At the same time the child may draw or paint another rabbit with long ears, eyes, four feet, and fingers on the end of the forefeet. The fingers and arms are functional in the picture because this rabbit is painting Easter eggs. It needs both arms and fingers to perform this task. The rabbit's eyes are also important because he must see what he is doing. The child is now in the stage where his work is recognizable to viewers.

A 5-year-old boy, Bill, carries out this idea of necessary details in painting an experience (Figure 4–3). The auto in which he had been riding had a flat tire and Bill was left in the car while his mother went for a mechanic. Important details were needed to express his experience, so he depicted himself behind the wheel of the car. He also painted the driver's seat where he had sat and guarded the car.

SEEN IN PICTURES

The pattern of growth in making pictures, as described above, is not typical of all children. Some skip one or more of these developmental patterns. However, the idea is to allow plenty of time for the child to experiment if he feels the need, and not to rush him from one period to another. Allow him time to get acquainted with the art media and at the same time discover his abilities and the possibilities of different materials.

A child finds it natural to express his feelings by painting, building, constructing, crayoning, and modeling. Often it is easier than talking if the child does not have sufficient words in his vocabulary or if his language does not flow smoothly.

The child needs to speak the proper words and understand their meaning to tell a story about some experience. When language is not at his command, the child has his art to tell the story for him. To be creative he must use concentration and problem-solving to depict a three-dimensional form in two dimensions.

As the child further observes things, he becomes more aware that objects he has been drawing have more details and parts. Take for example his characteristic tree which he begins to draw at an early age. This object is one of his first attempts at illustrating the world around him. This tree appears early in his search for self-expression, and is usually shown as a vertical line with a circle on top of it.

This concept of a tree satisfies the child until he grows in observation. He becomes aware that trees have leaves, branches, and thick trunks and his tree begins to take on a different look. Lines jut out from the circle to represent branches and his tree now looks like a rayed sun on a stick.

As the child grows, observes, and experiences objects and people his work is affected. Therefore, changes take place, sometimes slowly, sometimes quickly, depending on his experiences and observations.

Teachers see a great deal of the development of children in the end products they make. They find many characteristics or patterns that seem to be found in the work of most children.

importance of ME

Often in his art work, a young child makes himself the largest thing in the picture, regardless of what the picture contains. He may be shown standing alongside a tall building, but *he* towers over all other objects in the picture (Figure 4–4).

FIGURE 4–4
Picture Showing the
Importance of ME

This prominence of self in his work goes along with what is known of this young child. He is still in the stage where he is trying to find out about his environment and his place in the surroundings.

His language indicates this same tendency of his feelings of importance about himself. His sentences about his own activities usually start with, "One day ME and my daddy . . ."; "ME and my sister. . . ."

In his art work the importance of ME is usually displayed in the over-sized pictures of himself, while all other objects in the picture are minor or do not appear at all. The portrayal of self looms large and detailed.

disregard for color

Colors the child uses are chosen in various ways. Corcoran's[1] study on this subject differs from one done by Alschuler and Hattwick.[2] The latter

[1] A. L. Corcoran, "Color Usage in Nursery School Painting," *Child Development*, 25, No. 2 (1954), 107ff.
[2] R. H. Alschuler and L. W. Hattwick, *Painting and Personality* (Chicago: The University of Chicago Press, 1947).

point out that paintings of nursery school children show a relationship to the child's behavioral characteristics. Corcoran concludes that children choose colors in relationship to the position of the paint on the easel. The child, he finds, usually starts from left and uses colors from left to right in order of their arrangement. Other possibilities might be considered as to why children seem to disregard color. Let's look at a few ideas.

Liking For Specific Color. A child might choose to use a special color, regardless of its appropriateness, because this is the color he likes—his favorite color. So, a tree may be purple, a dog may be green, or a house may be black.

This trend for a love of color appears over and over in the child's work. If the color is not available, he may ask for it. He is like a woman who prefers wearing a specific color—it goes with his personality.

Laziness. The child may use a color which is not realistic because he is lazy. He knows all the colors he needs are in the back of the room on a table ready for his use. However, he is in the *front* of the room painting, and it is a long walk to the rear of the classroom.

So, he uses the colors he has on the easel or table where he is working. Even when the color he needs is near him on the table or easel, he may not want to bother moving or reaching to obtain the desired color. So, he uses a color within reach.

Depicting What He Sees. A child may not see colors as we expect him to see them. A tree that a teacher feels should be green, brown, yellow, orange, or red (depending on the season) may look blue or black to the child as he looks at a real tree in the sunlight or shadow. He draws as he *sees*, not what should be.

Lack of Supply. A teacher may not have many colors available, and only one container of each color. A child cannot always find the color he needs in crayons or paints if this setup is followed by the teacher. If the color he wants is not available, one cannot blame him for using what is there.

perspective and size

Nursery school and kindergarten children do not have an understanding of perspective. Everything in their pictures floats without a baseline for objects to stand on. If a teacher insists, they will draw a baseline for objects, grass, and sky—even a horizon—but this is only to please the teacher.

Objects, regardless of their position within the picture, float through space unless a track is needed for a train or a road is needed for an automobile. Even then, the track or road does not appear in perspective. It appears to be drawn from an aerial view. The tracks may be bigger than the train, while the train floats happily above its proposed guide line.

People, animals, and objects are drawn in respect to their importance in the child's mind, rather than in contrasting sizes. A dog will be larger than a giraffe which is standing (or floating) by the side of the dog. A flower will be larger than a house on whose lawn it grows. This is the way the child points out the importance of objects. He comes to school in the early spring and sees a jonquil growing. This becomes an important discovery. As he relays this experience through his art work, the flower takes on gigantic size to tell all of the child's discovery.

Another way the child shows his disregard for perspective is in the chimneys that adorn his boxy houses. They jut out the side of the roof in the form of a square with smoke pouring from the stack (Figure 4–5).

FIGURE 4–5
Typical Chimney
on House

The smoke from the chimney often curls across the entire picture. It can even complete a circle around the picture and return to its origin— the chimney. This is the large muscle development of these young children seeking release in broad, sweeping strokes. The child likes to draw long and vigorous lines and swirls, and through this activity may be saying to the teacher, "Give me more and larger paper—I need room."

interests relayed

A picture by a young child will often help a teacher discover the interests of the child. If he persistently draws within the same area of concentration, a teacher may have the necessary weapon she needs for helping the hard-to-reach child. He may be a reserved, quiet, unsocial being, but he loves to draw and paint pictures of ships and boats. If these pictures are displayed on the wall or on the bulletin board, it may cause his peers to question and praise the work. This could call for an answer from the artist. (The teacher can relay the compliments if the child is too shy.) It may be that this picture is the child's social entrance into a group who is interested in *how* he did it, or who wants to hear the story about it. Maybe the artist could demonstrate to a small group of interested children his techniques for creating such a picture.

ideas and understandings worked out

In order to understand what a thing means or what it does, a child will sometimes draw pictures of objects or ideas he is trying to understand. Or he may express something he has seen in order to make it clearer.

The child is taken to an airplane assembly plant. This is his first look at a *real live* airplane. This is his first time to touch and sit in a real plane. These machines now become three-dimensional objects instead of the two-dimensional ones he has seen in books. He is told to enter the small plane by stepping on the rubber part of the wing. No one tells him why, but he follows directions and places his small feet on the proper mats of rubber.

Once back in school, the child begins to assemble the information given on the trip. He draws pictures of the plane showing himself stepping on large black spots—the rubber stepping pads he has seen on the plane. In one drawing he is seen entering the plane, in another drawing he is seen leaving the plane, and in both pictures the mats are so large they almost cover the wings.

After completing his picture he asks the teacher, "Why did I have to step on just this part of the wing?" His art work, and the teacher's explanation have solved a problem for the child and added to his understanding of an experience.

copying

Children will sometimes sit side by side, and one child will copy the art work of his companion. There may be several reasons for this.

Seeking ideas.   The child who is copying may not have an idea of his own, and so is borrowing one that he sees and that is close to him. The theme of the two pictures may be alike, but the copied picture may vary in detail and in certain shapes. For example, the square windows of the original drawing may be depicted by the copier as oval or lopsided.

Admiration.   The child may copy through admiration of the other's efforts. He likes what he sees another doing and decides to make a picture as much like it as possible.

Praise.   The originator of the picture may have received considerable praise for his product, and the copier wants to have that same response from the praiser.

Symbol Search.   The child who is copying may be trying to perfect his own symbol,[3] and is picking up ideas from his friend. The child uses borrowed techniques, colors, or shapes to make his own symbol more realistic or more pleasing.

SEEKING APPROVAL

These young children love praise. They ask for it if it is not offered freely by the adult. Such questions as, "Is this right?" "Did I do it right?" "It's pretty, isn't it?" are often posed to adults.

A complimentary answer is all they need for acceptance or admiration

[3]James A. Smith, *Creative Teaching of the Creative Arts in the Elementary School* (Boston: Allyn & Bacon, Inc., 1968).

of what they have done or made. More than at any other age, this young child (especially at 5) wants to please the adult. One way to know he is doing this is to ask for approval.

REPEATING A PICTURE OR AN IDEA

If an adult praises a child too strongly about one of his productions or acts, this praised production will be duplicated over and over with the hope of gaining that same welcome response from the admirer.

Praise, in this case, acts as a detriment to the child's future work or ideas because, rather than try to add further details or changes, the artist or worker feels he has reached the peak of perfection in drawing or doing this specific thing. Why should he add any more parts to his creation? Why should he change from what he has done before?

UNFINISHED PICTURES

When a picture is started by a young child, he may often leave it unfinished or probably finish it some other day. This may be due to various reasons—some apparent and some known only to the child.

time

The adult may limit the child's time for production, assuming that creativity may be limited in time and that all ideas and thinking are done by a clock.

crayon

Maybe the crayon is limiting the child's creativity and attention by being almost entirely covered by paper. The child is unable to use the long side of the crayon, which would permit him to make longer strokes and to cover more space with less effort. The paper can be removed for better use of the crayon.

Perhaps if the child is 3 years old, he needs a crayon which has been chipped and melted into a large mold by placing it in the oven (see chapter 6, p. 60 for a way of making this type crayon).

brush

The child may be using a brush whose handle is too long and it may be difficult for him to control because of its length. A shorter handled brush might result in better control.

Maybe the brush head needs to be wider, thereby allowing the child to cover more space quickly and easily. Offering a variety of shapes and sizes of brushes would help to meet the individual differences and needs of the children.

fatigue

Maybe the child is just tired of what he is making and doesn't want to finish it (Figure 4–6). Isn't this also true of adults? A woman starts making a crocheted tablecloth. It takes a long time to complete or she may never complete it, through lack of concentration over such a long period of time.

The teacher must be sure that she is not demanding a finished product, if the child does not want what he has created. The demand may be for lengthening the child's attention span. The same thing could be done by encouraging the child with such words as, "I see you are almost finished"; "It's going to be a nice picture when you finish"; or "Do you need anything else to help you with your picture?"

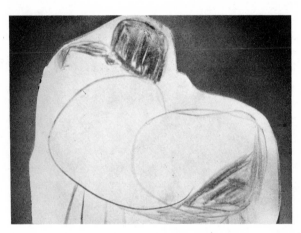

FIGURE 4–6
An Unfinished Crayon
Picture of an Elephant

An unfinished box, placed in the room, encourages children to place work they have not completed in this box and finish it another day. It may be necessary at times to ask children if they have something in the unfinished box which they could work on and finish.

SUMMARY

Yes, pictures made by the preschool child hold much of his development, experiences, likings, and wonderings. Pictures can tell the adult a great deal about the child if the pictures are not analyzed and directed.

Once direction enters the scene, creativity disappears. The child, in his eagerness to please, will add strips of blue sky, a line of green grass, a horizon, and a horse with all four legs. But, these are not *his* interpretations. He is following orders imposed by adults.

Left alone the child discovers *his* sky, *his* grass, *his* four-legged horse. This is accomplished through further observations, stories read to him, conversations in which he participates or to which he listens, and field trips.

A teacher must avoid worrying or diagnosing the child who persistently uses what the teacher feels is the wrong color. He may be using it from love of that color, from laziness, or from poor selection presented by the teacher. If teachers are ready to judge children, then they should also be willing to judge themselves.

5   the young child

his three-dimensional media

Most of the media that children use in the preschool groups are worked with in two dimensions. However, some materials are three-dimensional and give children an opportunity to create in width, breadth, and depth. Blocks, clay, wood, and sand are examples of such materials.

BLOCKS

One of the play materials every preschool group cannot be without is a good set of unit blocks. The name is derived from the medium's basic guide—an inch cube—which is the unit governing the size for all the other blocks, making them multiples of the inch cube. This assures a perfect fit when various sizes of blocks are used in the same structure.

The unit set includes squares, circles, rectangles, arches, pillars, and various halves and quarters of some of the forms. In addition to fitting well together, these shapes also offer the child arithmetic. This comes in the form of matching blocks, seeing how many blocks make a larger block, counting, and using arithmetical terms (see chapter 12, pp. 109–10).

In order to be inviting to children, any blocks should be displayed in an inviting manner. Here are some guide lines for arrangement and display.

displaying blocks

Blocks need to be in full view at all times so children will be inspired to use them. Placing them in closets, storing them in bins or boxes, or placing them in covered cases prevent this freedom of use.

Shelves for the blocks should be about as tall as the child's shoulders, should contain about three or four shelves, and should be in a part of the room where floor space is available for the children to build. The building space should not require the children to build directly in front of the shelves. Building too close to where blocks are stored does not allow freedom for others to obtain blocks. Having a space for building that is not too far away eliminates hauling and walking too far which could discourage some children from using the medium. This is especially true when it comes to pickup time. The shorter the distance, the more quickly the blocks may be put away.

ease of access

Blocks should be arranged so children can take them from the shelves without any trouble. This means that they cannot be stacked with the shelf space completely filled with blocks. There should be some space on the side and at the top of the shelf so little hands may reach in and grasp the blocks without too much effort or tugging.

grouping

The arrangement of the blocks should be such that all the large or heavy blocks are on the lowest shelf, while the smaller blocks are on the upper shelves. All the single units should be together, all the double units together, all the circles together, etc. The blocks should be placed so the size of the block can be identified before removing. For example, the long side of the blocks is displayed rather than the short end.

amount

There should be sufficient blocks so children do not have to wait for turns to use them. Blocks are usually one of the most popular of the play materials. There need to be plenty so children can build sprawling structures.

accessory toys

Small toys are a part of block-building construction. Small cars, rubber or wooden people and animals, pulleys, airplanes, and trucks are some of the things which encourage children to make a variety of constructions. These accessories become a part of the block shelf display, and are placed on top of the shelves or on a shelf by themselves.

suggestions

Blocks should be uncolored to serve as an unstructured play material. If they are colored bricks, children may always make brick houses when they build. If they are all red blocks, children may always make red houses, barns, and fire engines. Without color the blocks say to the children, "Make anything you want because I don't have to be a special thing."

These play materials are one of the most expensive expenditures of a preschool group. Therefore, it is wise to pay more and buy blocks made of hardwood, rather than those made with soft wood. Hardwood will last for years, whereas the soft wood can splinter and become rough with handling, scraping, and dropping. Hardwood blocks do not chip and do not scratch easily. They stand rougher treatment, such as toppling over.

Some children prefer using blocks at a table. The unit blocks are too large for this purpose, so a school may also like to purchase various types of table blocks, such as: colored cubes, Lincoln Logs, snap blocks, large dominoes, large tinker toys, or plastic blocks which hook together, slide together, or snap together. There are varieties of small blocks on the market. Small blocks can also be purchased in unit blocks.

If a teacher wishes to emphasize recognition of likeness and difference, she might like to trace the forms of the various blocks on the backs of the shelves. This designates the spot where the various sizes are stored, and children learn likenesses and differences in this manner. At the same time, blocks are always found in their proper places.

A child needs experiences to be able to express himself with any medium or play material. The teacher very often supplies these experiences through trips, visits, or having visitors to the school. How can a child make a farm scene if he has never seen a farm? How can he depict a garage if he has never been to one? How can he make a fire engine house if he has not had the opportunity to see a real firehouse?

These young children learn a great deal about their environment through use of their senses. They smell, taste, listen, and feel many things and make these a part of themselves and their learnings. Blocks give the child this same sensory satisfaction through the child touching, feeling their smoothness and hardness, and noticing that their hardness resists pushing. So, blocks must *feel* good to the child. Also, children like the noise of blocks. They will sometimes clap two blocks together to get a drum sound. Some children may even taste and smell the wood of the blocks.

WORKBENCH

"Oh, the noise when the children hammer and saw! It's just too much confusion to have a workbench in the room." This is the statement of some preschool teachers who may not look beyond the noise of the bench to realize the values children may gain through the use of this art medium.

First, a workbench makes a child feel grown up. He is imitating his father whom he has seen using tools. When the child is confronted with these same instruments for building, he becomes a little more grown up, a little bigger, a pseudoadult.

The muscular coordination and development, which teachers strive to foster in the preschool child, is well covered through the use of tools at a workbench. To hit a nail on the head a child must look and coordinate the hammer head with the nail head, using his eyes and hands together to make an accurate aim.

Socialization goes on at this art center. It is a small group of children because of limited space at the bench, but problem solving goes on as well as language development. Both of these experiences are brought about through association with peers, as they work side by side at the workbench.

This is a vigorous activity, for the most part, and is often needed as a release for the child after sitting or being quiet for too long a period of time. It is an especially good activity on a rainy or cold day when the program is entirely indoors.

The wood used at the workbench should always be a softwood. This is easier for the child to saw and nail. There is nothing more frustrating than to hammer and hammer, and not have the nail go into the wood because the wood is too hard.

The workbench often extends to social studies and science which may be going on in the room. In one kindergarten the children had been introduced to magnets and their workings. These magnets were left on the science table for use by the children, and for their experimentation. One day, after making a boat by placing a nail in the middle of a small piece of wood, a child took the magnet and pulled his boat across the room. His science learnings became a part of the art work, and what he had witnessed in the way of magnetism was being applied.

Yes, the workbench is noise. It takes supervision. It may even cause the principal to come to your room and ask for less noise because the next room is reading or studying. But one must look beyond the noise for what is *happening* to the children, and then it becomes a necessary art center for the young child.

rules

Workbenches must have rules for the safety of the children. These rules are important ones for the children to adhere to.

Tools. Tools must always stay at the bench. It is dangerous to walk around carrying saws, hammers, and nails. Children are told to leave all materials at the bench when they leave for any purpose.

Number Of Participants. Of necessity the number of children at the bench needs to be limited, depending upon the size of the workbench. One space, which holds the vise, accommodates one child because of the length of space needed to operate the saw. Children can stand across from each other when hammering, in an area away from the vise. Most benches can provide working space for about three or four children at a time. This means a standard size bench as described later in this chapter.

Vise.   When sawing, it should always be by placing the board in the vise. This prevents hands from being cut, which could occur when a child wants to hold the board steady. It also gives the sawer a firmer board to cut.

Saw.   Two hands are placed in the saw hole in the handle to avoid accidents to the child. This keeps both hands occupied so that it is not possible to hold the board that is being sawed. It also gives the child more control of the instrument—he has more power when he uses the strength of both hands.

materials for workbench

There are many kinds of materials which can be used at the workbench other than the usual wood, saw, and hammer. What is used depends on the maturity and ability of the children, and their capability in handling the tools.

Workbench.   Rather than buy a commercial bench, which is usually rather small, it is better for the teacher to have one built to her specifications. Most high schools will do this for the cost of the materials. The bench should be approximately five feet long by three feet wide, if room space permits this size. If space is not available in the room, then the bench could be placed in a large closet or in a hallway. If a separate room is used, perhaps the teacher would also wish to use this same space as a block building room. Then all the noise is concentrated in one area. It also encourages children to make things at the bench, which may become part of a block structure.

One type of bench that can be made is built of sturdy hardwood, with a beading placed in the middle of the workbench to hold the nails (Figure 5–1). This center nail holder keeps the nails from bouncing all over the bench as the hammering is done.

Tools.   The tools should be man-sized ones. Children's toy tools do not do a good job and are frustrating. Children get very tired and discouraged trying to get these playthings to do what they want them to do. Hammers are so light the nails cannot be driven into the wood. Saws are so dull they will not cut.

Hammers are bought by weight, and saws can be obtained in various handle and blade lengths. The main thing is that the tools must *work*.

Nails.   Nails should be of various lengths, but all should have large heads. The head must be seen by the children, so the larger the better. It is also easier to hit a large-headed nail.

Various lengths of nails aid children in problem solving. They must decide which length of nail is right for the special piece of wood they are using—which nail will not come through the other side of the board. They must measure.

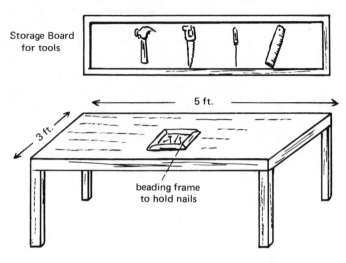

Storage Board
for tools

5 ft.

3 ft.

beading frame
to hold nails

FIGURE 5–1   Homemade Workbench

Extra Materials.   Once children master the use of the hammers, various
other materials may be added to the workbench for use by the children:

1. Pieces of cork for nailing onto wood;
2. Soft drink bottle tops for nailing onto wood;
3. Pieces of cloth for gluing to wood for boat sails, or up-
   holstery for chairs;
4. Corrugated nails for use in nailing two boards together
   when placed flat on bench and side by side;
5. Pieces of styrofoam cut into small pieces for gluing or
   nailing to wood;
6. Empty cotton spools;
7. Pipe cleaners for gluing onto wood;
8. Uncovered wooden button molds to be used as wheels.

Extra Tools.   Hammers are usually presented as the first tool for children
to use. Then the saw is added to the workbench. As children reach the age
of 5 there is usually a need for measuring, which means a ruler or measuring tape is added at the bench. Screws and screw drivers are also added.
These take a little more coordination and a different kind of manipulation.
It is a good idea to have children try them out by screwing them into some
soft object, such as styrofoam, until the boys and girls get the idea of
working the screw driver.

CLAY

Another three-dimensional art material is clay. This gives children an opportunity to explore the possibilities of molding in height, width, and depth.

During this preschool period, the child is not particularly concerned with *making* something. He is mostly concerned with manipulating the clay, learning its feel, experiencing its pliability smelling its earth odor, noticing its response to patting, pulling, twisting, squeezing, rolling, and shaping.

Most schools use the unmixed powdered clay because of its inexpensiveness and also because children like to mix their own clay. Watch the young child as he prepares his own clay. He squeezes it between his fingers with enjoyment. It is patted, pushed, and rolled while the child's hands and arms become covered with a mud pack. Here are the mud pies that all children love to make, but are so often prevented from making.

Clay offers opportunity for the child to see differences in shapes and forms. It also helps the child notice contrasting proportion in objects— larger than, smaller than, taller than, shorter than.

Once the clay is ready for use, the child approaches it in a step-by-step process of investigation. His first delight comes from pounding and flattening the medium. This is done with zest and he will sometimes say that he is angry at it, or that he is making a pancake. However, for the most part, he enters the experience for the sheer joy of pounding and seeing the change in the material. Michelangelo must have had this same feeling of elation as he watched the rock change into *David* or *Moses*.

The child's next step might be rolling the clay by placing it on the table and rolling it with the flat of the hand. This results in what the child terms "snakes." He not only rolls them but will wiggle them over the table. He might even chase his friends from the table, by using the snake as a threatening agent. Snakes continue to fascinate him for some time.

As he works with the clay, the child is learning that this art form can be shaped quickly into a form, which may be changed almost miraculously by a push, a touch, a squeeze, or a drop. So, although he starts with a ball-shaped form, it can be changed into a flat plate by pushing or pounding. A flat plate becomes a snake with some rolling.

Then the child may become aware that by rolling the clay in larger pieces, he can make balls or ashtrays. He may even make a birthday cake that calls for candles. These touches can be supplied by using small sticks, or pegs, and the cake is ready for a song, a party, or destruction.

props for clay

Tables need to be covered when clay is used, and the old reliable newspaper or kraft paper is the best. These can be thrown away after the clay work is over, and the cleaning up takes little time. These working papers are taped to the table to prevent the paper from sliding, and to allow for the vigorous work of the artists.

Saving large cardboard pieces provides the teacher with good clay boards for each child. Cardboard, such as is found in men's shirts when they come from the laundry, is fine to use for this purpose. The bottoms of large boxes are also good disposable working boards.

If the laundry cardboards are used, the clay does not stick so readily if the work is done on the shiny side of the cardboard. An object made on this board may be left to harden on the molding pad, after which the board may be thrown away. Again, there is no cleaning or scraping of boards—no washing to do. In this age of gimmicks and time-saving devices, even the preschool teacher joins the social trend in conservation of time and effort.

A small quantity of water placed in a low container on the clay table will provide children with a smoothing agent. They may use this when they want their product to be even and contain no bumps. By dipping fingers in the water and then going over the clay product, the desired smoothness may be obtained. (Avoid offering too much water, as some children like to mix clay with more water. Overzealous children may turn clay to mush.)

Smocks are a *must* because of the possibility of getting clay on the clothes. An easily made smock is one made of two large turkish towels sewn together at the shoulders. These slide over the children's heads and are also good for painting, as the paint does not come through the toweling as quickly as it does through smocks made of cloth. The paint also does not run off at the bottom of the smock as it could with plastic smocks.

A small round ball of clay—about the size of a tennis ball—makes an adequate working piece for each child. If a large amount of clay is placed on the working table, children will either collect or hoard the medium. They may also be overwhelmed by the large quantity available, and the space it takes up on the table. They may just decide to accumulate the clay in piles in front of them, and not use it for making things. So, each child receives a small amount, and is given more if his product requires it.

accessories

Other objects may be presented with the clay after the child has passed the experimental stage and is beginning to make things. Any of the following may be used, but not too many at a time. These stimulate different uses of the clay.

1. Paints for dry objects;
2. Rolling pins;
3. Yarn;
4. Tongue depressors;
5. Buttons;

6. Plastic knives and forks for cutting and designing;
7. Acorns for making prints;
8. Wax paper or aluminum foil. Offer children this paper while they are using clay. Have them mold their clay object with the paper wrapped around the lump of clay. They will see the ridges the paper makes in the clay when the paper is removed. They will also see the smoothness the paper has created.

uses of finished products

When products are completed, have children tell stories about the thing they have made. It may not look like any specific thing, but so much the better. The child can then use his imagination to bring this object to life through telling a story of what he thinks it is, or how he feels about it.

Place completed objects on a special table and have an "Art Exhibit." Label the object with the artists' names and have the exhibit for the next PTA meeting.

Use shoe boxes (placed on their sides with the lids removed) and you have a display case for various pieces of art. Maybe each child would like to have his own "show window" display.

storing clay

When children have finished with the clay, the teacher may roll the leftover pieces into small balls about the size of a tennis ball. Placing a thumb on the top of the ball, push a hole into the clay about half way into the ball. This hole is filled with water, and all the clay is placed in a flat container and covered with a damp towel. The liquid keeps the clay from hardening, and water can be replaced as it is absorbed.

variations of clay

A variation in the type of molding material provides the children with different textures, each offering a different feel and smell.

Plasticine. This is a nonhardening clay and is not too easy for the very young child to manipulate. It could be kept on hand for those who are capable of using it. A disadvantage is that the children cannot take it home, as it is kept soft with white vaseline and is used over and over again.

Ivory Snow and Water. This is made by mixing the Ivory Snow with water, or with water containing food coloring. Mix this with the hands until it is the consistency of clay. Children like the smoothness and slippery feel of this type of clay. Placing a small container of water on the working table helps children smooth out rough places in their molds. If coloring is not used, children can use their molds for a home bath.

Sawdust and Wheat Paste. This is a rougher texture than the soap, but still pleasing to children. It cannot be molded too thickly, or it will not dry properly. Drying can be hastened by placing the product in a slow oven until the water is evaporated. (See chapter 8, pp. 75–76 for recipe.)

Papier Mache.   Tear newspaper or newsprint into small pieces and add hot water. When paper is completely wet, squeeze out the excess water, and add wheat paste so that the mixture forms a malleable clay.

This makes nonbreakable objects when it hardens. If it is molded too thickly, the object may mildew. To be safe, place a hole in the bottom of the molded object. This allows for circulation of air which hastens drying. Turn the object from side to side as it hardens.

Flour and Salt Clay.   Mix two cups of flour with three-fourths cup of salt. Add water which contains food coloring, and the children can roll this out and cut out forms. It can also be molded into shapes. At Christmas time, the children can cut out cookies, using cookie cutters. While the dough is still soft, punch a hole in the clay near the top of the cookie. When the cookies are dry, paint them and place a string through the hole. Then hang all the cookies on a Christmas tree. (Make the dough thin when cutting, so the product will not crack as it dries.)

Cornstarch Clay.   Mix a cornstarch paste by cooking cornstarch and water until the starch is dissolved. Let the starch cool until it thickens slightly. Add tempera paint of the desired color, and let the starch thicken until it is usable for molding.

SANDBOX

An indoor sandbox is another form of material which can be molded. The sand must be sprinkled with water each morning, so that children can make three-dimensional pictures in the box. The sand can be changed seasonally. In the winter, especially during the snow season, the sand could be white sand; in the other seasons, the sand could be the usual brown color.

Sandboxes can be changed in other ways. Instead of sand, substitute any of the following for a different texture and a different kind of use: large shavings of wood, salt, mud, small pebbles, rice. Not all of these can be molded, but it is also fun to have things just for measuring and for pouring.

SUMMARY

Blocks are valuable for mathematical concepts, for distinguishing likenesses and differences, for creating horizontal or vertical structures, and for creating designs of various kinds. They are also of value for giving a child a general feeling of accomplishment when he has completed a building which is his own idea, his own creation, and his to use as he wishes. At times, he may even wish to place a sign on his structure asking people not to take it down. As one child had the teacher print for his building,

"This is a nice building. Please don't take it down. I want to use it tomorrow."

If a teacher looks at the values a child will get through using a workbench and its tools, then she forgets about noise. She looks at the development of the child. However, if the noise is still a little too much for her to endure, she may place the workbench legs on cork, or on a thick mat, to deaden the sound. A teacher must always keep in mind that the workbench is an art medium and, along with clay and blocks, is an opportunity for the child to create in three dimensions. The teacher must also remember that all children are not ready for workbenches. She must be aware of the children's readiness and maturity. She looks first for the children's responsibility toward the group and toward themselves. Are they hitting, pushing, and grabbing? If so, they are not socially ready to use tools which could become hitting weapons, and thus, are dangerous tools. Look first to the social adjustment of the group.

Clay is malleable and pleasing, and its feel is a fine sensory experience for children. Its possibilities and creative outcomes are satisfying to the young child. It is one of children's favorite media. They make forms and often name them—forms which could be most anything, but which children choose to label with their own choice of names.

6   the young child
his other art media

In addition to three-dimensional media, there are other media used by children in the nursery school and kindergarten. Tempera, finger paint, string, collages, crayons, chalk, and styrofoam are among a few of the materials to experiment with.

All of the above media require paper, with the exception of styrofoam. It is interesting to vary this paper, instead of offering the child the same shape and kind day after day.

PAPER

For the most part, young children like large paper—large enough to allow the painter or drawer plenty of room to make large bold strokes. At the same time, the largeness of the paper allows for the big muscle development of the child—an important development at this age.

variations in paper

There are many ways to vary the paper that the child uses. Here are some of them.

Shapes. The standard square or rectangular paper can be varied by

offering the artists other shapes—round, triangular, diamond-shaped, oc-
tagonal, and star-shaped. These different shapes usually cause the child
to follow the contour of the paper. Because of this, he will make curves
and angles. Using the usual rectangular and square paper, he might make
just straight lines, up and down.

The paper shapes may suggest different forms if put in different positions from time to time. For example, a triangle may be placed on the easel,
or the table, by having the base of the triangle at the bottom. The next
time, it may be placed with the base at the side, and at another time have
the base at the top. A rectangular or diamond-shaped paper may be placed
with the longer side going vertically one time and horizontally at another
time.

With these different shapes the child may possibly *see* and *produce*:

1. An Easter egg from an oval-shaped paper;
2. A tree from a triangular paper;
3. A valentine from a heart-shaped paper;
4. A balloon, face, or ball from a round paper;
5. A sailboat, a pennant, or a tent from a triangular shape—
   depending on the position of the base of the triangle as
   it is placed on the easel.

Sizes.   There may be further variations in the sizes of paper offered the
child. Try using strips of adding machine paper. The young child sometimes likes to make tiny pictures. A strip of paper such as this could remind
him of making "millions of things." Make some strips long, some short,
and offer these along with larger paper of varying lengths and widths.

Texture.   A variation of textures will acquaint the child with the ease of
some papers and the resistance of other types of paper. Sandpaper, oily
paper, manila paper, shelving paper, corrugated paper, second-sheets of
typewriter paper, and any other paper that can be marked upon give the
child an understanding of the ease or difficulty of applying an instrument
to paper.

Paper that is cut from strips of corrugated paper that is packed in boxes,
or colored corrugated paper that is bought by the roll, may be cut into
squares, circles, triangles, or rectangles. These may be presented as one
kind of material on which to paint or crayon. Some children like the in-
dented spaces on the corrugated paper and may follow the lines, which
gives them a controlled eye-hand coordination movement. Some will notice
the difference between paint and crayons. The crayons will dent the paper,
whereas the paint will not, unless the child bears down very heavily on
the brush.

This corrugated paper could be painted on, and then the painting could
be imprinted on another paper while the paint is still wet. The children
might also enjoy using two or three of the paintings and applying them

one on top of the other, until all three paintings have been imprinted to form one picture. This is done by lightly pressing the pictures together.

PAINTS

Variation in paints often stimulates children to experiment and create different pictures. Other than the usual liquid tempera, the following could be introduced.

dry powder tempera

Sometimes children enjoy using powdered tempera without the addition of water. With a brush and can of water the child can dip the brush into the water, and then pick up some of the dry tempera with the wet brush. The tempera—very small amounts—can be placed in divided aluminum dishes.

This is a good way to conserve paint. If only a small amount of water is placed on the brush, the painting will be much more vivid than when liquid tempera is used.

bon ami or other window cleaners

The liquid form of some window cleaning materials is a different kind of paint. The pink type cleaner makes pretty pictures on black paper. Or, if the school allows it, have the children use this medium to paint the school windows with designs. The custodian may appreciate the removal by the children, and the windows will be cleaned for him.

roll-on painting

Tempera paint, mixed to a slightly thick consistency, may be put on paper in one of two ways.

Rolling Pin. Using a large cardboard tube, or a rolling pin, apply the paint to the roller and then roll across the paper. The paint may also be dripped on the paper and then rolled on. These often turn out pretty enough to use for wrapping paper for presents.

Deodorant Bottle. Another form of roll-on painting can be done by using a deodorant bottle. To prepare the container for the paint, carefully remove the plastic ring around the ball of the bottle. Take out the ball. Mix paint to a slightly thick mixture, and fill the bottle half full. Replace the ball and plastic ring, and the children may use the bottle to roll designs on paper or cardboard.

homemade paint

Boil the following in water and you have a makeshift paint in case the school supply is running low:

carrots	light orange
dead leaves	tan
beets	pink or red
spinach	light green
crepe paper	small pieces make light shades

mixing paints

To make the mixing and cleaning of paint cans easier, fill paint jars with cellophane bags. Paint may be mixed in the bags by shaking. The bag is then inserted in the jar, with the top of the bag over the outside of the can. Close the jars at night by pulling up the top of the bag, and placing a rubber band around the top of the bag. This keeps out the air and prevents the paint from drying. If the bags are hole-free, your paint jars will also be paint-free, and no washing is required. The bags may be thrown away and new ones substituted.

brushes and other instruments for painting

Have a variety of brush sizes from which children may choose. Some children like large brush heads, some prefer small ones. Some like long handles, some like short handles. Even small brushes, such as those used in painting small furniture, find a use in the preschool group. Just be sure the brushes will fit the jars or cans. The children will take care of the rest.

On occasion, why not vary the instrument used for painting? Instead of brushes, encourage children to try small pieces of sponge attached to sticks.

Brush Containers.   It is important that the ferrules of brushes be protected from water soaking. Brushes should be hung with the brush end down as they are drying.

For a container for this purpose take a large piece of rubber tubing and place it on a framework of wood. Punch holes through the tubing and board. (Make the holes a little smaller than the thickest part of the brush handle.) Insert the brushes by pushing upward until the tubing holds the handle (Figure 6–1).

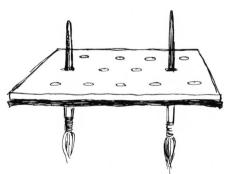

FIGURE 6–1   Brush Container

Brushes also may be hung, brush end downward, on a board in which holes have been drilled, and round elastic stretched from one hole to another to provide a hanging space for brushes.

Another type of container may be made from a large tin can. Punch holes in the bottom of an open can, making them large enough to hold the brush handles. Hang the can, open side up, and insert brushes from the bottom. A piece of tubing, placed across the end with the holes, will give more security for the brushes.

Another possibility is to use a board about three feet long and about six inches wide. Glue snap clothes pins so that the snapping part hangs over the edge of the board. When the snap is released, a brush can be held in the pin so the brushes can dry. This can be nailed to a shelf so that children can place their brushes in the pins after washing them.

paint containers

One argument, usually raised against floor painting, is that paint jars are difficult to manage when they do not have the security of the easel box. Let's look at some ways in which a certain amount of security may be assured.

Board Container. Why not try placing paint jars in a thick board, with circles carved out to fit the paint jars or cans? If the holes are deep enough, the board can be carried with ease and without spilling.

Soft Drink Container. Some teachers use soft drink cartons to hold paint jars or cans. Fruit juice cans are just about the right size for this purpose. This is an easy piece of equipment to carry because it has a handle and is also light weight.

Easel Safety. If your school insists on easels, try taping the jars or cans of paint in the easel box. Place a large strip of masking tape around the container and secure the ends of the tape to the back of the box. This technique helps avoid spilling of paint.

EASELS

What are the disadvantages of using easels? In the first place, they are expensive. In the second place, they allow only one or two children to paint at a time.

Would there be more advantages for the child if he painted on the floor? First the child has more arm room to use paper and paints. His body can take many positions, such as reclining, sprawling, or sitting—typical positions for the young child. Secondly, the floor affords an opportunity for larger social groups, especially if the painting process is allocated to one part of the room. The paper can be larger, which in turn offers more room for more children.

FINGER PAINTING

A young child not only finger paints, he becomes a part of his creation. As his hands glide through the wonderful feel of the paint, his whole body seems to be involved in creating the picture. Sometimes his arm becomes a part of his "production," as elbows and sides of arms join in the fun of making a picture.

The child's body closely hugs the paper as he rubs, scrubs, or gently draws the paint over the slippery paper. Here again is a sensory experience that is well-liked by young children.

No matter what the child makes, the "masterpiece" is attractive. So, he doesn't feel compelled to make any special thing—lines, fingernail marks, knuckle marks, and palm marks blend together in a lovely design. This is one art material in which the child's body is in direct contact with the medium. There is no brush, no sponge, no instrument of any kind between him and the paint. He becomes a part of the paint and paper.

The table on which finger painting is to be done should be prepared ahead of time. This is done by taping newspaper or newsprint firmly in place, so that the child's vigorous motions will not move it from the table. The piece of finger paint paper should be large to satisfy the child's need for using large broad strokes. The paper, if wet on both sides, will not curl so readily when it dries. The water will also help the paper adhere to the table cover.

A little water added to the finger paint will help keep the picture wet while the child is working on it. This is better than a teacher dropping water or squeezing a wet sponge over the child's product to moisten it.

Sometimes it is exciting to have two or three children work on separate pictures, and then, place their wet finger paintings one on top of the other with the paint sides together. This transfers one painting onto the other and makes a depth picture. Two or three such transfers, using different colors, makes a pretty picture. The transferred picture will be slightly different from the original as only the raised paint transfers.

Another possible picture can be made by children using a spatter screen, and placing it over the wet finger painting. Using a piece of chalk the child can place a spray of chalk on his picture, which gives it a sparkly appearance.

variations of finger paint

Finger painting may be varied by using the following mixtures instead of the usual commercial paints. However, the writer has found in working with all types of finger paint that nothing takes the place, or has the lovely smell and feel, of commercial paint.

Salt And Flour Mixture.   Mix two parts flour to about one-fourth part salt.

To this add enough colored water to form the proper consistency. Tempera may be used as a coloring agent.

Soap-Starch Mixture. Mix one-third cup of glossy laundry starch with two cups of boiling water. Add one-half cup of soap flakes. Another way to make this would be to use two cups of detergent with one cup of liquid starch. Watch for children whose hands may be allergic to soap.

Ivory Snow And Water. Mix enough water with Ivory Snow to form a mixture which is slightly thick. Color may be added by using vegetable coloring.

Powdered Paint. Spread liquid starch over paper. Then, using a large salt shaker, shake powdered paint over the surface of the paper and finger paint the two together.

Cornstarch Paint. Mix two cups of flour, one cup of sugar, and one cup of cornstarch to a paste by adding a little cold water. Pour boiling water over this until it thickens. Stir the mixture until it becomes clear. Add vegetable coloring or tempera. The sugar gives the paint a glossy finish.

If a teacher is aware that children use their vivid imaginations in a variety of ways, she might like to tape a large piece of paper on a table top, and have the children finger paint on this stable background. Once completed, the picture may be examined by the children for things they would like to talk about. What can they see in the picture? This is language development. How many reds do they see in the picture? This is counting. What story can they tell from this picture? This is creative writing.

Occasionally there may be a child who wants to finger paint, but doesn't want to get his hands in the paint. This is rather rare because most children want to get their hands in this medium. If such a thing should occur, the child might like to use a toothbrush instead of his fingers. The results are rather pretty and different.

As the teacher works with the children, she may want to encourage them by saying, "Have you tried using your knuckles?" "Have you tried your fingernails?" "Have you tried the back of your hands?" "Have you tried the side of your hand?" This makes different marks on the paper and gives the children a variety of ways to use their hands, instead of using just their fingers. Watching the young child as he uses the paint, one would wonder why it is called finger paint!

Some teachers like to have children finger paint directly on a table. Then, the paintings are picked up, by placing a piece of paper over the work and rubbing lightly before picking up the paper. This gives a reversed picture of the work that was done.

STRING PAINTING

Give paper, string pieces, and paint to the young child and see the results. But first, have a little discussion:

Teacher: Today, we are not going to use brushes when we paint. Instead we are going to use pieces of string, like this. Now, how could we paint with this piece of string and this thick paint?

Harry: I know what I'd do. I'd hit the paper with it and make marks.

Teacher: Good idea. Remember, Harry, when you try this you will have to watch and make sure no one gets splashed with your paint. What other way could we use this string for painting?

Mary: Make it in a ball like this (she squeezes string into a small bunch). It would make some kind of mark.

Helen: You can drop the strings on paper after you put paint on the paper. Oh; No brush. Anyhow, I could use my fingers and finger paint the paper.

John: I would get the string painted and then put it on the paper.

Teacher: How will you paint the string, John?

John: Just put it in the paint.

Fran: You know what? You could just wiggle the string on the paper and it would look like snakes.

Teacher: We have some good ideas. Let's try painting the way we want to try, and maybe someone will have another idea.

RIBBONS

Small pieces of grosgrain ribbon, or heavy satin ribbon, may be used for making "beauty" pictures. The ribbon, plus glue, plus wood or cardboard, is enough material to have children experiment with this medium. The finished pictures may be covered with Saran-wrap and make nice pictures for Mother's Day presents.

TISSUE PAPER AND GLUE

Thin tissue paper may be torn into jagged pieces and glued to a piece of wood. First apply Elmer's glue to the wood; then place a piece of the tissue paper on top of the glue; and then, apply glue to the top of this paper. Layer on layer causes the object to take on a look-through aspect, which is as likeable as a masterpiece. Plastic bottles, heavy cardboard, or styrofoam may also be used instead of wood.

GADGETS

Gadget painting can be tried with all kinds of miscellaneous materials found around the house or school. A clothespin, buttons on sticks, a pastry blender, plastic forks, corrugated cardboard on a stick, toothbrushes, open ends of plastic bottles, and roller-type hair curlers are just a few of the possible materials. If the paint is mixed to a creamy mixture, the gadget prints will not run when applied to the paper.

CHALK

Chalk is one of the media which is the most difficult to apply without smearing, either during production or after the work is completed. Some of this smearing may be avoided by wetting the paper with a sponge and then applying the dry chalk. This process also makes a brighter color than that acquired by using dry paper. (Beware of using paper that is too thin and will tear easily when water is used.)

If a slippery surface is required, liquid starch may be applied to the paper before coloring with the dry chalk. There is less friction in using the starch. Children will find it easier to apply and, at the same time, the colors will be bright.

Soaking pieces of large chalk in sugar water (one part sugar and two parts water) for about fifteen minutes, and then using dry paper, is another way to apply chalk. Sugar gives the chalk a shiny look when dry.

Covering each piece of chalk with a piece of aluminum foil, and leaving about one-half inch of the chalk exposed, will prevent smearing. It will also prevent the transferring of colors from one chalk to another while they are stored.

Thick pieces of chalk are preferable for small hands. It is possible to purchase large chalk in square or round form. The square is less likely to roll off the table.

COLLAGES

Making a collage can be a rewarding experience. Any kind of arrangement, any kind of material, and any kind of paper usually result in an interesting picture. Nothing definite has to be made—just an arrangement of the materials. Cardboard makes a nice background for applying the materials. Another background which offers more flexibility is burlap.

materials for collages

Elmer's glue makes most items adhere to the above background materials. Along with the glue and background material, offer the children about five or six of the following items (too many from which to select may result in confusion on the part of the child) *buttons, beads, rick-rack, ribbon, string, yarn, candy wrappers, small pieces of aluminum foil, pieces of cloth, bias tape, small twigs, shells, pebbles, small pieces of macaroni, rice, sand, sawdust curls, feathers, salt, pipe cleaners, paper doilies, and nut shells.*

These small items take hand-eye coordination and muscular control to manipulate. Further coordination and control can be provided by furnishing the children the glue supply in shallow dishes, with a Q-tip for an applicator.

After some experimenting with collage work, try giving the children something other than paper, cardboard, and burlap as a background. On the table, display the collage materials along with the following: *box tops, small cigarette boxes, cigar boxes, styrofoam pieces, plastic containers, small wooden berry boxes, and plastic bottles.*

See what happens to the collage materials when other than a flat background is offered to the group. It may result in beautiful flower arrangements, people, trains, and other things.

Q-TIPS

Q-tips offer practice in fine muscle coordination. They should be chosen with care because the tips come with wood, plastic, and paper stems. Be sure the stems are wood or plastic, or the tips will break with a small amount of use.

Present the Q-tips to the children with a small quantity of liquid tempera. Some children will like the smallness of this type of painting. Others will prefer a throat swab, because it is easier to hold and manipulate. It also covers more space in less time than the Q-tip. Having both sticks on hand satisfies the needs of all.

Q-tip holder

If children enjoy using Q-tips for paint, try making a holder for your paints as follows.

Use two tongue and groove boards, each about a foot long and six inches across. Glue the tops of small medicine bottles to the boards (top side down) and insert the glass vials in the tops. This device may be used as a unit, or the boards may be separated if paint is used in two areas of the room.

CRAYONS

Crayons are an art medium familiar to most children. Many shy children prefer using this medium because of the security they feel sitting at a table, away from any aggression in more active parts of the room.

Some lazy children use crayons, particularly because of the easy pickup they afford. There is no scrubbing of tables, no washing of brushes—just a few tosses of the crayons into the box and then placing them on a shelf.

kinds of crayons

There are wax crayons and crayolas. The former offer less resistance and are used on paper or cloth. Removing all paper from the crayons gives the child a chance to use the sides of the crayons, as well as the point. A large crayon is preferable to a thinner one, and gives the child a firmer grip and mastery of the crayon.

displaying crayons

Most teachers, when purchasing crayons, will buy a box for each child in the group. However, only half of these boxes are placed in the art corner during the first six months of school. The rest of the crayons are brought out for use when the first crayons have become broken and too small.

It is possible to leave the crayons in their original boxes or to use cheese boxes made of wood. Each box is painted a color of some crayon, so that each color is represented by a box. Crayons of a corresponding color are placed in the appropriate boxes.

melted crayons

A teacher can accumulate all the broken pieces of crayons, and make one large crayon for the children's use. This is done by making a container (in any desired form) by smoothing and bending aluminum foil. A small aluminum dish may be used, if it is not larger than a small child's hand.

In these forms, the leftover wax crayons are shaved. Then, the container with the crayon shavings is placed in a slow oven and, as the crayons begin to melt, a toothpick or small stick is used to stir the crayon.

When the crayons are fully melted, set the form aside for the crayon to harden. Once hardened, the form is taken out. With this type of crayon, the child's small hand can hold the object more firmly and comfortably. Another advantage is that the child has many sides to use when drawing— the thin sides of the crayon for small lines, the broad side for quick bold strokes, and the rough top for different markings. (The rough part is the top of the crayon as it melts in the oven.)

STYROFOAM

Styrofoam is easy to find. It is used as packing in most electrical pieces and certain types of bottles; hospitals or doctors might save it for a school.

Broken into small pieces, styrofoam almost tells the child what to make with it. The dents and cuts on the large pieces of foam can be cut to suggest certain forms.

A supply of gadgets near the foam may give the children ideas. Try old golf tees; old pegs; bottle tops; yarn; twigs; and any other object that can be stuck into the foam.

WIRE

The next time the telephone man installs a telephone, he may leave pieces of telephone wire on the floor or in the wastebasket. Save these! Children can use the pieces to make shapes, forms, and figures. They like its ease in bending and twisting.

SPATTER PAINTING

There is very little creative thinking when a child spatter paints. If he is given a design by the teacher, which he produces by using a screen, then he is merely copying something which has been made for him. But if the child is asked to make his own picture by tearing the construction paper into any shape he wishes, then he has created his own design. This design can be placed on a piece of paper and covered with a spatter screen. For a brush he can use a vegetable brush, which seems to work better than a toothbrush. This brush is rubbed all over the screen to produce an outline of the picture on the paper. When the picture is removed, the outline appears.

One of the difficulties in this type of work is the difficulty, for the child, of keeping the screen in place and keeping it from sliding. The following design for a homemade screen is made for the purpose of keeping the screen anchored in place while the child is working on it. Its other advantage is the largeness of the screen, which allows for more arm movement.

spatter screen

Make spatter paint screens from discarded wooden cigar boxes or wooden cheese boxes (Figure 6–2). (A 12" × 12" size is best.) Place

FIGURE 6–2   Spatter Screen

rubber weatherstripping on the sides of the bottom of the box to prevent slipping when the screen is being used. A small scrub brush can be used for applying the paint. (The farther apart the hairs of the brush, the less dripping.)

MURALS

The term "mural" is interpreted to mean "an expression of one or more persons, using one or a variety of art media, based on experiences, ideas, or imagination of the creator or creators."

What inspiration brings about a mural?

Surely the teacher does not say, "Today, boys and girls, we are going to start a mural about all the things which help us to travel from one place to another." Nor does the teacher paint part of a picture on a large sheet of paper and ask the children to finish her idea. What, then, is the beginning of a mural?

Sometimes a mural is inspired by a large blank sheet of paper hung on the wall in a conspicuous place. A child may make something, and the teacher may suggest that the child place the picture on the large sheet of paper. Once started, others will want to join in to help the mural grow. The teacher may suggest that a particular child might like to work on the picture the group is making.

She further stimulates interest by placing extra "things" near the developing mural—pieces of cotton, lace, sawdust, ribbon, sticks—or materials that may bring about new ideas or that may advance ideas already started. For example, if the children have been interested in making trucks or buses for a mural, the teacher might like to place some green Easter basket filling nearby in the hope that some child or children will see the possibilities of making grass, trees, or flowers.

Such a classroom mural began one day when a boy said, "I can make a picture of the airplanes we saw yesterday." This first airplane produced other airplanes, and all the "productions" were placed on a large piece of paper. The contributions varied—some children painted, some crayoned, some used tongue depressors, some used clay. But one boy's idea had inspired the group, and the teacher was there to correlate the thinking.

Another example of how a mural can begin took place after a kindergarten teacher had finished reading about a little boy and his breakfast. A boy said, "That's a lot of pancakes. How many is it?"

The teacher asked how the group could find out what that many pancakes looked like. One child said he had seen pictures of pancakes in magazines. The teacher suggested that some of the children might like to cut out all the pancakes they could find, or, if they wanted to, they could draw them. She hung a long narrow piece of paper on the wall from ceiling to floor and the children began to paste on their pancakes.

The interest grew as the pancake pile grew. The teacher made sure that brown and yellow paints were available, that round pieces of paper were on the art shelf, and that the children were reminded now and then that the pancake pile was almost completed. When it was finished, one child was heard to remark, "Willie couldn't have eaten all that many." Arithmetic—fiction—language. Art develops many concepts.

Sometimes the teacher can motivate children to begin a mural by asking the group if they would like to show the children who missed a trip, some of the things the group saw. "We didn't have a camera to take pictures, but we brought back pictures in our heads. Maybe some of you would like to draw or paint these pictures and we can tell John, Mary, and Helen about the things we saw. There is a large piece of paper in the back of the room where we may hang our pictures."

What do we need to do a mural? A large box or container to hold the paints and brushes; sponges for painting large pictures (the sky, grass, etc.); large kraft paper placed on a background of oilcloth or newspaper to protect the wall; newspapers to protect the floor; extra media for adding to the mural (these might include materials such as crayons, crepe paper, thin wood, wood shavings, construction paper scraps, facial tissue, and cotton).

The best murals seem to be those in which the children draw or paint pictures to paste on the large paper. This gives the children the freedom to choose the picture they wish to add to the production. It also gives them the opportunity to choose between displaying the picture or taking it home.

SUMMARY

Whatever the media presented to children, they should be displayed as compactly and orderly as possible. If there are many small things, small tin pans will hold them and, at the same time, separate and categorize them.

Let the material suggest a use to the child. He doesn't need to be told to do something with it. Place it on a table and the child is soon hard at work.

Regardless of how many media are available in the classroom, teachers should not feel that *all* children should be interested in *all* art media. This is not a realistic idea if one remembers that each child is an individual, with his own interests, likes, and dislikes.

Regardless of stimulation, regardless of suggestions, each child undoubtedly is going to prefer certain media over others. Some children will not be interested in handling a specific medium. Some children may be allergic to a certain medium. Each individual has his personal and justifiable reasons for his preferences. This is why teachers should be certain that a variety of choices are presented to children, so that selections may be made and all children will not have to do just one thing.

Teachers must get away from the idea that all children enjoy making a snowman which the teacher has patterned, that all children need directions as to how to make something, that all children are neat and should always present a perfect product, that a teacher's idea is always the right one.

If we keep in mind that what is happening to the child as he uses the medium is more important than what he produces, then teachers are working in a creative manner with the preschoolers. What are his learnings as he draws, paints, models, and constructs? Does he learn that paints change color when mixed? Or does he learn that drippings of paint can be controlled? Or is he learning to work with others on a project or building? Or is he doing some problem solving as he works?

What do children need in order to be creative?

They need SPACE, space, space—room at tables, space on the floor.

They need MATERIALS—plenty and varied so that borrowing and waiting are not necessary and choice is possible.

They need TIME—to finish work once begun. Forget the stop signal when artists are consumed by the creative urge.

They need FREEDOM—to express themselves and their ideas rather than those of the teacher.

They need EXPERIENCES—to give them concrete ideas to express.

The results of providing these media and opportunities will be rewarding to the teacher and stimulating to the children as creators.

7   the young child

his music

As in all facets of the preschool program, exposing the young child to music has many behavioral objectives. Basically, children get a great deal of pleasure through singing and responding to music. This then becomes one of the objectives—sheer enjoyment. Music does "have charms to sooth" and, therefore, another objective might be the releasing of tension, or the quieting influence of special music.

Another goal might be to have children learn something from the song or music. It might be the sequence of the song that the teacher feels is important for children to be exposed to. They listen to the tune so they can respond in accordance with this sequence. It may be that concepts are a part of the song—a shape, a distance, an animal. There is also the possibility that some songs or rhythms might be used to stress change in tempo, making the body respond fast on some sounds and slowly on others.

Children are exposed to music in a variety of ways. Here are some examples.

MUSIC APPRECIATION

Just listening to music for the beauty of it, for the rhythm of it, for the soothing effect of it, is offered at some time in the program. Sometimes a record is played, or the teacher plays the piano or another instrument, and the children listen for specific things. When do they hear the cat walking softly? When does the dog growl? When do the children dance? Children listen for these sounds and then discuss them.

Sometimes instead of asking children to listen for specific things, the teacher will ask the children what the music said to them. Often it is their own interpretation of the music and not the way the teacher would have interpreted the selection.

Music appreciation of a quiet, soothing type is sometimes used during rest time. Children can stretch out on their cots, or blankets, and close their eyes and see what pictures they can envision as the music is played. It is fun to discuss it after the rest. Stories sometimes evolve this way that are worth recording and putting on paper for future reading.

Another resting technique that includes music is for the children to listen to familiar songs played on records or the piano. At the close of rest, the children gather together and tell what songs they heard played. As they identify the various songs, everyone sings them. This gives children something special to listen for, and a special recognition when he tells of the song he heard.

Appreciation may also be encouraged by asking the children to bring in a record of their own that they feel other children would enjoy. The teacher could specify a nonsinging record so that the boys and girls will have an opportunity to figure out what the music is saying.

RHYTHMS

Music can also help children express the mood of the rendition by responding with their bodies. If each child finds a space in the room where he will not be touched by someone else, he will have a private place to do rhythmic interpretations. (This is less negative and less suggestive than saying to the children, "Let's get someplace where we won't hit anyone.")

It is hoped that each child will respond in a different way, according to the way the music affects his body movements. The teacher might try saying, "Let's see what the music tells each of us to do." Then she might say, "Let's see how the music makes our arms go" "What does it tell our shoulders to do?" "What does it make our fingers want to do?" using different parts of the body for each playing of the rhythm.

The teacher should remember to compliment the individual differences as the children do rhythmic movements. Instead of requiring a specific response to a given piece of music, encourage individualistic movements. "Look how many different ways we can move to that music!" "All of us are doing what the music tells each of us to do," might be her encouragement for divergent thinking and acting.

It is interesting at times to let the children set the tempo of the music. By using two sticks, a drum, or two blocks, the child can start a rhythmic beat. All the other children can carry out this beat with their bodies or some part of their bodies.

Some kindergarten report cards show the following category in a form similar to this:

Music And Rhythms

	Very		*Needs*
Ability to skip	*Good*	*Fair*	*Help*

How many 5-year-olds have mastered skipping? Probably about one-half the class can skip, or can do a hopping-jumping combination. The other half may not try or may do a gallop, a hop, or a run. Imagine mother's consternation when she sees "needs help" after her 5-year-old son's skipping ability! She would probably have him practicing at home to change that report card to a satisfactory mark.

One way to help children skip is to play some skipping music, but not mention the word "skip." To the tune of the skipping, the teacher sings a song about each child—what he is wearing, what he did today, what color his shoes are. The words might be, "John is wearing black shoes, black shoes, black shoes, and he's going round the room." The music will sometimes bring on a skipping movement if the rhythm is stressed. Children are so interested in listening for their names, and the accompanying recognition, that they do not think of what they are doing.

DRAMATIZATION

Young children also enjoy acting out a song or musical tale. These are simple little songs that tell a story. They can easily be made up by the teacher on the spur of the moment:

> Boys and girls, listen to the story and then you can be the one who is doing all these things. One day a nursery school child went to the shoe store with her mother. Her mother bought her a new pair of brown sneakers. The child put one shoe on one foot and the other shoe on the other foot. Then she walked down the street. First she walked slowly, then on her tiptoes, then on her heels, then backwards. As she walked she stepped in a big mud puddle and her shoes were covered with mud. She ran home and took off one shoe, then the other shoe. She put the shoes on the floor to dry.

As the story is being told, the teacher can play music which is the appropriate tempo for the various parts of the story. Each action should be given enough musical background so that the actions are not too close together.

A simple story about a slide could also be used:

Let us climb up the steps of the big slide. Careful! Hold onto the railing of the slide. Now we are at the top. Let's sit down and wait for the piano to tell us to go down the slide (slide the hand across the keys from right to left). Now we are down.

MUSICAL INSTRUMENTS

Young children are not naturally orchestra-minded. They want to experiment with the instruments, and listen to the various sounds they produce. So, instruments are placed on display for the use of the children.

However, the teacher may incorporate the instruments in a music period by having each child hold an instrument, and listen for the name of that instrument to be called. This, then, means it is time for that child to play with the piano or record. With the melody shown in Figure 7–1 the teacher

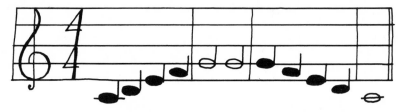

FIGURE 7–1   Rhythmic Melody

might sing such words as, "Listen to me playing, playing on my drums— sticks—bell—block."

Or, the teacher may take such a song as *Skip To My Lou*. It may be sung and the instruments played at the time their names are mentioned. The song can be replayed for each instrument, to offer more opportunity to use the instrument.

The drums are playing, boom, boom, boom.
The drums are playing, boom, boom, boom.
The drums are playing, boom, boom, boom.
Listen to their music.

The bells are playing, ting-a-ling.
The bells are playing, ting-a-ling.
The bells are playing, ting-a-ling.
Listen to their music.

The sticks are playing, click, click, click.
The sticks are playing, click, click, click.
The sticks are playing, click, click, click.
Listen to their music.

The blocks are playing, (click with tongue).
The blocks are playing, (click with tongue).
The blocks are playing, (click with tongue).
Listen to their music.

Everyone is playing, playing softly.
Everyone is playing, playing softly.
Everyone is playing, playing softly.
Listen to our music.

TEACHER-MADE MATERIALS FOR MUSICAL EXPRESSION

In place of expensive musical instruments, substitute sturdy homemade ones. There are many possibilities for making a variety of these instruments. These are just a few.

tone blocks

Insert a stick in the open end of a juice can (6 ounce size). Nail the stick to the closed end of the can. Fill the can about one-third full of rice. Tape the stick to the open end of the can by placing masking tape completely over the opening until the stick is firmly in place. Cover the can with contact paper or paper stripping. When paper stripping is used, paint and then design or decal the can after it is thoroughly dry.

Make about six or more of these instruments, placing different materials in each can—pebbles, nails, sand, small bolts, carpet tacks, thumb tacks, noodles, macaroni, or any other articles that will make a noise when the can is shaken or hit. The idea is to expose children to differences in sounds of the various shakers—some soft, some loud, some high, some low.

sand blocks

Using a piece of wood about four inches by five inches, place coarse sandpaper on one side, securing it with thumbtacks. Place a small door knob on the other side, and then shellac all but the sandpaper.

Make this in duplicate. The two blocks can be rubbed together to make a musical instrument. Using thumbtacks makes it easy to replace the sandpaper when it is worn out.

shaker

Using two small sieves, place beans in one of them and then cover it with the other sieve. Tie these together securely, and then cover with paper (tissue paper and Elmer's Glue make a nice covering—about five coats of paper). This makes a nice shaker and is very attractive to children.

drum

These are rather difficult to make so that the sounds are good. One of the best ways is to use an old wooden nail keg or larger wooden barrel, if desired. After sanding and painting, buy an old drumhead from a music store and pick out the best part. Wet the drumhead with water and stretch it taut across the keg by placing wire around the keg to hold the head in place. For drumsticks, buy two dish mops and cover them with cloth or leather. Be sure to drill small holes on the bottom side of the keg to produce a sound that is not hollow or muffled.

tambourine

Using two embroidery hoops, wire bells or bottle tops on the outer hoop. If bottle tops are used place two tops together, back to back, so that they will hit each other when shaken. Between the two hoops, place a piece of wet chamois which is stretched tightly and held in place by the overlapping of the hoops. If the hoops do not hold the chamois securely, sew it in place by connecting the sides of the chamois with long heavy threads.

triangle

Bend a sound, solid curtain rod into a triangle, leaving the open ends a little apart. For a striker, use a small piece of the curtain rod. (Before making this instrument, test the sound of the rod when hit. Some rods sound better than others.) Place a heavy cord on a closed part of the triangle, and the child can hold this as he strikes the triangle.

SUMMARY

Music should be a part of the whole day in the nursery school and kindergarten. Children sing as they work, sing as they play, sing as they talk. They sing, sing, sing. Many of these children make up songs—melodious little tunes that do not always rhyme but that contain the child's feelings about some object, event, or person. These improvised renditions could become a part of the songs of the school.

Music means singing, expressing melodies with the body, and listening to the moods of records, instruments, and orchestras. Music is a magic wand that draws children like the pipe of the Pied Piper. It is wonderful to watch the faces of children as they respond, in song or motion, to the "music in the air".

Dramatization and use of instruments and improvised songs by the teacher are further facets of the music in the preschool. Children should be encouraged to add to their musical experiences by bringing in records or music books, or singing a song they have learned and want the others to hear.

8   the young child

his puppets

Puppets can be very valuable to the young child. They now appear in most nursery schools and kindergartens as a toy for use in dramatic play. Children also use them to express an experience, an idea, a feeling, or they use them as a therapeutic measure. A puppet becomes what the child wants it to be—himself, his parent, his friend, an imaginary personality, or an animal. In addition, puppets give the child a chance to create with his mind and hands, thus giving him a mental and physical exposure to an art medium.

USE BY TEACHERS

What value do puppets have for the teacher? Let's examine a few ideas of how the teacher may use puppets in the nursery school and kindergarten.

clarification of words

The classroom teacher uses puppets to aid the child in understanding a concept, a story, or a feeling. She will read about a dog who hid *in back of, in front of, alongside of*, or *under* the chair. These spatial concepts are clarified by the dog puppet being moved (by the teacher or children) to the appropriate position with respect to a chair. Children, in this way, are learning the meaning of the words as they watch the motions of the puppet.

The teacher may read, or bring about discussion, regarding the boy who *jumped, hopped*, or moved *quickly* or *slowly*. The children see these motions as the teacher moves the puppet in accordance with the words. All of these clarifications of words aid the child in later reading. When he encounters these same words in print, he will remember them through past experiences.

decision making

Another use of puppets has to do with classroom decisions. A child brings in a book that he wishes read to the class. On that same day, three other children have brought in their favorite stories and also wish the group to hear them. Which book should the teacher read?

Instead of the teacher deciding, she uses the puppet as the decider. The names of the books are placed in a basket or box, and the puppet "draws" a name from the container. In this way the teacher is not being the one to decide which book is to be read, and she is not placing value on a special book or favoring a special child.

language stimulation

The teacher also uses puppets to stimulate language. She may present a new puppet to the children and ask them what they would like to say about this new toy. Children will speak freely about its likeness to something or someone they know. They will speak about how it is used. They will even go into creative language, as they make up a story for the puppet.

This is the beginning of creative writing and the teacher may record the story. To make it a part of the class she can print this story, bind it, place an author's name on the front (Author: Kindergarten Class of Stone School), and make this book a part of the children's library or browsing corner.

cover for shyness

Children who are shy will usually speak freely if they have a puppet in their hand. The attention of the group is on the puppet, not on the child. Knowing this, teachers can encourage oral participation by having many kinds of puppets available for the children.

The teacher also knows that using puppets helps to develop expression. She hopes that this expression will be carried over into the children's reading in first grade.

emotional release

There is always the possibility that some children will need to express anger, tension, fear, and other emotions. This can be done with a puppet so that the child does not feel *he* is the one doing the expressing. He is like the adult at the Mardi gras—he is being someone else, and is not open to personal evaluation or criticism.

attention to rules

Teachers may also use puppets to bring something to the attention of the group and, at the same time, help to explain the reasons, or rules, for this particular thing. Children may not be following the rules which are made for their safety. The teacher uses the puppet to point out the methods and reasons for doing things in a required way. The children who are not following rules are not singled out as wrongdoers, and those who are following rules have their learnings reinforced.

foreign children

Puppets are a wonderful play activity for the child of foreign background. The teacher can introduce the child to various puppets, and these can be used by the child to express what he cannot say. The fine thing about puppets is that they aren't required to talk. Actions by the puppets speak louder than words and help other children understand what the foreign child is trying to say.

CREATING PUPPETS

What kinds of puppets can be made by the young child without too much help or direction from adults? If the child has the muscular coordination and control of materials, he might be exposed to the making of certain types of puppets.

child-made puppets

Given the proper materials, time, and freedom to create, the child can make usable puppets—ones that give him satisfaction. Here are some of the easier kind that he might be able to make.

Paper Bag Puppets. These are easily made by drawing a face or form on a folded paper bag (large enough to fit over the child's hand or even his head).

When the design is completed, the bag can be stuffed with wadded newspapers or smaller paper bags, and placed on a stick. However, the child might like to use the bag over his hands when he operates it.

If the puppet is worn over the child's head, eyes should be cut in the proper place in the bag. The position of the eyes is measured and marked by the teacher, then cut out by the child.

Plate Puppets. Using paper plates as a head, children can draw any design they wish on the inside or outside of the plate. If strings are attached to either side of the plate, it can be worn as a mask. Or a stick may be glued, or taped, to the plate to make a stick puppet. For children who want more reality, the teacher should provide cotton, wood shavings, crepe paper, ribbons, and buttons for use as hair, neckties, features, etc.

Plastic Can Puppets. These are made by covering a small plastic container with paper. Tissue paper is easy to apply. Simply add a little water to Elmer's glue. Apply bits of paper to the can by brushing on the glue mixture, then brushing on the bits of paper. (Instead of using a brush, Q-tips may be used.)

Features may be added, or bits of construction paper may be used for facial parts. Operate on two or three fingers, from the open end of the container.

Paper Cup Puppets. A sturdy paper cup will make a puppet which can be used by the child by placing it over his fist, or fingers. The unglazed cup is best because materials will adhere to the surface.

A face may be pasted on the cup, crayoned on the cup, or painted on the cup. Pieces of paper of various shapes may also be glued on the cup to form features.

Box Puppets. Save all small boxes—toothpaste containers, lotion boxes, and medicine boxes. These make tall, thin puppets, and can be manipulated by using two or three fingers in the open end of the box.

Pieces of cloth may suggest clothing to the children, and can be glued on the box. With a face cut from a magazine, a box puppet is ready to operate.

Paper Roll Puppets. Using rolls from toilet paper, wrapping paper, or paper towels, cut the proper size for the child to make a face on the roll (Figure 8–1). This puppet can be manipulated by using two or three fingers in the opening of the roll. It does not take as much coordination as the puppets that require a child to use fingers for the head and arms.

Ivory Snow Puppets. Mix Ivory Snow and water until it is the consistency of clay. Children model heads or animals and place a stick, or a finger hole, in the base of the head for manipulating the puppet.

FIGURE 8–1   Paper Roll Puppet

This is a good sensory experience because children love the feel of the slippery soap. It molds easily and dries hard.

Mitten Puppet. A child can apply features to a castoff mitten and use the product as a puppet. The mittens, with their furry look, often suggest an animal such as a rabbit, dog, or cat.

Other Puppets. Styrofoam balls, plastic balls, and rubber balls can be made into puppets by adding features and making holes in the bottom of the ball. They can be manipulated with the fingers or can be placed on sticks.

teacher-made puppets

If the teacher would like to save some expense, she can create her own puppets, an advantage being that the puppets can represent figures the children can use and understand. Here are some inexpensive ideas.

Box Puppets. A small shoe box (that comes with infant's shoes) will make a walking animal puppet. Using only the lower part of the box, make two finger holes in the short end. Fingers are placed in these holes and become the legs of the puppet. Decorate the box to resemble a person or an animal, and the children will use them in their dramatic play.

Stocking Puppet. A long, thick stocking is easy to manipulate as a puppet. When placed over the hand and pushed far up the arm, the stocking takes on character.

If a moving mouth is desired on this puppet, the teacher may cut the toe of the stocking and add an inner lining for a mouth. This will operate when fingers are placed at the upper and lower portions of the mouth.

Plastic Bottle Puppets. Many interesting puppets can be made using old plastic bottles (Figure 8–2). These may be placed on sticks or worn as masks by children. Children like the idea of *being* a puppet instead of just *using* one on their hands. It is also a good way to overcome shyness.

Ice Cream Container Puppets. Gallon cardboard ice cream containers can be made into life-size puppets that can be worn over children's heads for dramatic play. They also make good spacemen's helmets.

Paper Stripping Puppets. Starting with a wad of newspaper, strips of narrow newspaper can be applied to the wad by dipping the strips in liquid starch (diluted with a little water). As strips are applied in layers, the form becomes malleable and can be pushed or dented. Features can be applied by adding extra "lumps" of wadded paper to the form.

These puppets are very durable and a variety of these cost nothing (or very little depending on the kind of costumes added to the head). The top layer of the paper on the puppet head should be unprinted newsprint, or paper toweling, so the object may be painted on clear paper. (The newsprint will show through unless the paint is very dark.)

Sawdust Puppets. Sift very fine sawdust until it is like sand. Add water

FIGURE 8–2   Plastic Bottle Puppets.
Courtesy of Bethesda-Chevy Chase Cooperative
Nursery School

to this and squeeze it through the sawdust. Leave the excess water in the sawdust, and add wheat paste to make a molding mass.

Form this mixture into desired shapes but do not make them too thick— the wet sawdust may mold if it dries too slowly. (This may be overcome by placing the product in a slow oven and drying it.)

These puppets paint easily and are very sturdy. If an animal is made, a fork may be drawn over the wet form to give an impression of hair or fur.

Finger Puppets.   These are made by placing a decorated roll of paper around thimbles (Figure 8–3). These are placed on the child's fingers and manipulated by moving the digits. They may also be made by gluing faces or figures on plastic thimbles. If a quantity of thimbles is not available, apply the picture with masking tape, and the same thimble may be used for many different puppets.

Shadow Puppets.   The teacher places a large sheet in the room so it hangs in front of a window where the sun is entering and shining on the sheet. The child takes some objects behind the sheet and moves them to make a shadow on the sheet.

The sheet may also be used with the children themselves being the puppets. Each acts out his idea behind the sheet, while the other children guess what he is doing or being. This can be done after a field trip; children can act out the various things they saw. This is good for shy children, or children with speech difficulties.

FIGURE 8–3   Finger Puppets

PUPPET STAGE

A puppet stage is seldom needed for young children. They do not require everything to be realistic as they will in later years. Here are a few improvised stages that require no storage, no curtain, and no scenery.

table stage

A table turned on its side is an adequate stage for children's puppets to entertain. The child is hidden behind the table while he holds the puppet in the air so it shows over the edge of the table.

block stage

Another stage may be made by the children by using large blocks. These are piled high enough to hide the child, but low enough so he can reach the puppet to the top of the blocks.

piano stage

If there is an upright piano in the room, this may also be used as a stage. Children operate the puppets from behind the piano, using blocks to stand on if the piano is too high. The puppets are operated over the top of the piano.

box stage

For stick puppets, the teacher can construct a theater by using a cardboard box with one side open. Across the top, or bottom, of this box the teacher can cut a long slit, which will permit the sticks to operate through them.

This kind of equipment does not take up valuable classroom space which is so necessary for these active, vigorous children.

SUMMARY

Puppets should be a part of every nursery school and kindergarten. When the child makes them, he uses his creative abilities to express his ideas. At the same time, he is learning the feel, the possibilities, and the difficulties of various materials.

Using either his own product or one made by the teacher, the child can express himself verbally, emotionally, and physically. When he wants to avoid blame or ridicule, it is safer to have a puppet speak for the child. He can always blame the puppet for the wrong word, the wrong act, or the wrong feeling. There are times when everyone likes to hide behind a mask and be someone other than himself.

Expensive play materials can be inexpensively made by the teacher. They can last a long time if they are made sturdily. The children do not require a puppet dressed elaborately or in fine clothes. What the child gets from using the puppet is the important thing, not the beauty of the puppet.

9   the young child

his stories

Picture books are an important activity for preschool children. Books should be displayed openly in a well-lighted section of the room so that children can sit and browse through the pictures.

BOOK CORNER

The book corner becomes a part of the free play, or worktime, of the program. Children look through the books, examine the pictures, find pictures of articles they are trying to name, and learn to handle the books carefully and correctly.

After reading a story to the children, the teacher makes this book a part of the "library." Once they know the content of the story, boys and girls will take the book and read the pictures. Sometimes they read to each other as they watch the happenings of the pictures.

This corner may also be used as a "research" place. Children may bring in some article—flower, leaf, stone, or some other item they want to know about. The teacher can refer them to picture books showing articles in colorful form. When the child finds a comparable picture of the article he has brought to school, the teacher reads what the page says about that article.

Some schools use storybooks as a part of the rest time. Prior to rest, each child finds a book which he wishes to look at. This book is taken to his rest mat where he stretches out on his stomach and looks through the pictures as he quietly reclines.

Books are changed frequently to follow the current interests of children, to introduce a special addition to the room (for example, a new animal), or to follow the seasons. This keeps the reading center an interesting and stimulating place.

By using a public library, a teacher may add to the shelf of books in the school by borrowing literature for two or more weeks. Libraries are liberal in allowing teachers to take a large quantity of books at one time.

The book display may also include books (or stories) that the children have made and illustrated. These are bound, the covers illustrated, and the author's name added.

It is interesting at times to have the children bring in their favorite books, and have just their books on display. This offers children an opportunity to bring their interests and selections to the classroom for others to enjoy. It also makes the addition of books an important part of the program.

Further use may be made of the book corner by having a circulating library. Children take the book of their choice and keep it overnight, bringing it back to school the next day. This gives a child a responsibility for the book and also a responsibility to the group. He is asked to take a book belonging to the group, but the group wants the book back the next day so others may borrow it. This borrowing has resulted in the young child asking his mother for a library card at the public library.

The regular book corner may be extended to the house corner so that children can read books to their pretend families. As one child said while reading to another child, "Pictures are for children to read. The black stuff at the bottom is for adults who can't read pictures." Give the children opportunities to read the pictures and at the same time, let them become aware of that "black stuff" on the page.

READING BOOKS TO CHILDREN

There are thousands of books written each year intended for children's pleasure and education. Some of these books are great, some are good, some are fair, and others are not always suitable for the age group for which they were intended. Pictures may be overcrowded with details, words in the story may be beyond the child's understanding, or the illustrations may be too small.

Book lists appear all the time—from libraries, bookstores, educational organizations, and colleges. These list carefully selected readings, but do not always suit every group of young children. It is the teacher, herself, who has some influence on the book that is read. First, she must like the story she is reading to the children, or else she may read it too quickly and without enjoyment. Reading such as this may not let the children receive the full benefits from the book.

Second, each group of children will vary in maturity, background, and interests. These variations are a deciding factor in the types of books teachers select to read to children. Books that please one group are not always the favorites of other groups, nor are they appropriate for them. The teacher is often surprised at the stories that some children seem to enjoy and will request over and over.

VARIATIONS IN PRESENTATION OF STORIES

Stories may be presented in a variety of ways, other than by reading. Too often the teacher becomes so dependent on a book to tell a story that she does not remember that different ways of offering the stories to children will add interest and variety. At the same time, she is showing children that there are many ways of relating a story.

telling

Reading from a book is rather confining for the teacher. When she no longer has a book in her hands she is better able to see the faces of the children, watch their expressions, and watch the effect of the story on the listeners. This helps her become aware of what is happening socially or physically to the group before her. Is John about to hit Mary and cause a disturbance in the group? Is Helen gradually trying to inch her way to some other spot in the room? Does Harry look as though he is not feeling well?

Telling stories also allows for any additions or omissions which the teacher may like to make for the benefit of the group. This might not be wise if she were using a book in which pictures could point out omissions or corrections. This is assuming, of course, that the story she is telling is not a familiar one which, if changed, would call forth a reprimand from the children.

flannel board

Using a flannel board also allows for more teacher attention to the group. It also allows for participation by the children if the teacher gives them figures to add to the board as the story unfolds. This is especially good with the 2- and 3-year-olds who always want to be a part of everything that is going on.

In place of flannel a teacher may make figures from felt or pellon. Pellon is the best material for adhering to the board. Pipe cleaners are also good for making outline figures and look three-dimensional when applied to the flannel.

opaque projector

Enlarging pictures in books by placing them on the opaque projector is another way to tell stories. This enlargement brings out more of the details of the object, and also makes it easier for all the children to see. The group will not have to sit so close to the teacher to focus on a small book.

dioramas

Constructing dioramas and using them to tell the story is another way to have children see three-dimensional figures. The figures are placed in an open box and objects are added as the story is told.

films

Check the public library about films that are available for the young child. Again, this way of showing pictures in the larger form gives children a better understanding of the details of the figures.

pictures

Use pictures from an old book and mount these on colorful paper. As the story is told, hold up pictures that correspond with the lines being read. A jacket of a book might be used, as well as a single picture which tells a complete story.

drawings

Stories may be told by using chalk drawings, crayon drawings, or by drawing stick figures. It is easier, if the teacher is not a good artist or a quick one, to place faint pencil drawings on the paper before starting the story. This facilitates the telling of the story, as it is easier to quickly cover the existing lines.

phonograph records

There are some very good stories told on records. The teacher can use these and either have the children listen or show pictures as the record plays.

tapes

Having a tape recorder on hand is sometimes good for taping the stories children relate. These can be used for the story time, instead of reading from a book. The teacher might like to record a few stories herself. These could be used by the substitute teacher when the regular teacher is out of school. Children will recognize the voice immediately and feel that the teacher has not forgotten them and is with them, if only on a tape.

wooden figures

If the school has small figures made of wood or rubber, these may be used to illustrate a story instead of using the pictures in the book. They may be held by the children or the teacher.

scrolls

The teacher can make a sequence of pictures on a scroll. Oilcloth is good for a background, and oil paint will make permanent pictures on the cloth. As the teacher tells the story, she unfolds the scroll to show one picture at a time. The scroll becomes a part of the book corner after it is read.

musical stories

There are some stories in music books that can be used with the children. However, the teacher may play the piano (or any instrument) as she reads *any* story using sounds to represent characters or things in the story.

story board

Boards for telling stories may be made by the teacher with little effort. Cut out a series of pictures and glue them on a large piece of tagboard. The quantity of pictures depends on the age of the group. As the teacher reads the tale, she points to the objects about which she is reading. This also exposes children to the top-to-bottom, left-to-right concept of reading, as they watch the teacher point to the sequence.

magnetic board

A magnetic board may also be used for storytelling, if the teacher places magnets on top of objects which she places on the board. If the school has a quantity of magnets, the pictures may be glued to magnets and then applied to the board.

tv set

It is easy to make a TV set for the classroom. A large box, with a window cut in the front and an open back, becomes another way to tell a story. Using puppets or paper figures on sticks, the teacher can manipulate the characters as she tells or reads the story. This TV becomes a part of the play materials the children use and a selection of stories may be kept close by, or hung on the side of the TV. Place each story in a manila envelope with a picture on the front of the envelope designating the story.

children's pictures

Using pictures made by the children, the teacher may make up a story about them (with the permission of the artist). However, it is better if the child makes up the story about his picture, and the teacher reads it to the group.

TECHNIQUES FOR PRESENTING STORIES

By listening to the teacher reading, telling, or in some other way presenting a story, the child gains a reading background which will be valuable to him when he learns to read in the first grade.

holding the book

When reading a book, the teacher must be sure the children can see the pictures. She holds the book at waist height, with the pictures toward the children. This means the teacher must read by looking at the book from the side, or she could memorize the story.

If pictures are to be used for presenting the story to the children, then the pictures must be visible at all times—not just for a quick glimpse. They are valuable only if the children can examine them, and observe the relationship of words to pictures.

reading

The teacher reads slowly and pronounces each word clearly so children will hear the words correctly and without slurs in the words. The value to children is the vocabulary building through proper pronunciation and introduction of new words.

position of children

The reader usually sits on a low chair that allows her to hold the book at the children's eye level. If the book is held too high the children will be looking up the page instead of looking straight at the pictures. This could give a distorted view of the picture and an incorrect idea or concept. In the proper position they gain a clear and accurate view of what is being read, and can better envision the story.

tone of voice

The same tone of voice becomes monotonous as children listen to adults reading to them. This may cause the children to become restless. The teacher should always read with expression, changing her voice to suit the moods of the story—reading faster for a line that indicates faster pace, using a slow voice for lines that indicate a lagging or slowing down process, reading happily or sadly when the story requires emotional feelings of this type. Children thus experience the part expression plays in reading. The book comes alive!

concept building

The teacher may occasionally point to things in the picture to draw children's attention to the meaning of the words in the story. This clarifies concepts or clarifies the story.

handling books

Above all, because the teacher likes the book, she shows her regard for it in the way she treats the pages as she handles the book. She turns pages carefully. She does not bend back the cover or pages of the book. She does not wet her finger to turn the pages. In this way children understand the teacher's love for books, and are further influenced by the manner in which she handles the book with care—children learn that books are to be treated well.

STORY CONTENT

What kinds of books do children in nursery school and kindergarten enjoy and ask for over and over again? There are certain types of books that teachers could add to their libraries, knowing that most children would be happy and eager to listen to them over and over.

stories about children

Boys and girls love stories about other children, especially stories in which the characters are doing things that the listeners could not do—but would love to do.

They particularly like stories about children who travel on airplanes acting as pilots; stories in which children change personalities by donning different clothing or assuming different actions to suit the theme of the stories; stories in which children overcome obstacles and become successful despite failures.

Children also enjoy books that tell of children doing the same things that they themselves do—going to the beach, going to school, riding on buses, going on train rides, visiting relatives, or attending the circus.

suspense stories

Also well-liked are stories with an element of surprise that keep the reader wondering. What is in the box Daddy sent home? What is in the barn in the nest? What will happen to the little girl who is hiding in the leaves?

However, these nursery school and kindergarten children like the suspense solved at the ending of the book, and do not like the story to go on once the mystery has been solved. Once the solution is reached, children are relaxed and ready to stop listening.

humorous stories

Young children enjoy humorous stories. They like it when bears are chased by bees, when a dog runs away from his bath, or when a cat hides on a roof and no one can find him. These are usually stories in which the laugh is on the person or animal—a story in which some joke is played on a character.

The boy who pretends to be a fish and is almost thrown in the water; the boy who enters a whispering town and everything and everybody whispers until he awakens them to noise—these are the kinds of tales which bring smiles to the faces of the young child, as he listens to the silly antics of others.

animal stories

There are many children's books based on the activities or experiences of animals. These are always favorites of children, even if the animal is dressed and acts like a human.

real stories

Occasionally children like stories about themselves or about the teacher. These could be told, or drawn, by the storyteller. Telling children of an incident in the teacher's childhood is usually interesting to groups. (Children don't usually think of their teacher as having been any age, except the age she is today.)

repetitive stories

Find a book in which a phrase or poem appears many times. Before too much of the story is read the children will catch on to the repeating part, and will say it along with the teacher. Choral speaking in the making!

SUMMARY

Children are usually ready for a book to be read to them. The magic words "story time" generally bring the group together without any further coaxing.

An important part of the reading of books to young children is the opportunity it offers for discussions about the story. This usually follows the reading, and is preferably not done during the story. The interruption of a story may not permit the group to retain the theme of the tale, and the teacher must help the children recall what the story was saying when the interruption caused her to stop. The teacher may interrupt her story long enough to clarify a word or a situation, but then she should continue immediately.

Just getting children to listen to stories is not enough. The teacher must be aware of her pronunciation, enunciation, and expression, as she unfolds the story to the preschoolers. Her joy of reading, her care in handling the book, and her interpretation of the story create an atmosphere that can be absorbed by children.

Books should be a part of the daily activities of the children. These books, on display at all times, encourage children to browse. As they browse they will see that there are many kinds of books—different stories, different kinds of pictures, different sizes of books.

10   the young child

his oral language

"Hey, you know what?" is the beginning of many conversations the young child introduces. After waiting for the "What?" to be asked by the listener, the child begins to recount experiences, ideas, or stories which take many forms. They can be real or imaginary; they can be exciting, calamitous, or funny. It is the boy or girl expressing himself through his language.

Teachers, knowing of this great desire of children to express themselves and be heard, allow plenty of time during the day for children to talk, talk, talk. This goes on from the time he comes into the schoolroom, until he leaves for home. Often the language still flows as he enters his transportation for the homeward ride.

There are various provisions made for this free-flowing language of nursery school and kindergarten children. These provisions are supplied by the teacher, as she plans her program for the children.

GREETINGS

Most children, as they enter the room, immediately seek out the teacher to tell her of something special. This is a busy time for the teacher. If she can find the time to listen to each language outburst, as the different children approach her, she is providing the children with an opportunity to test the effectiveness of the language, as well as giving children a growing confidence in their communication.

FREE PLAY

This is a time when language can flow freely. If children are given play materials or art materials that bring about socializing, then language will be used. At least, language will be used freely if the teacher remembers not to talk too much herself. Often a teacher feels she must keep the conversation going, or that she must have the children learn by listening to her talk. If they must listen to the teacher about three-fourths of the day, they have little chance to do their share of the conversation.

Toys that need cooperative effort to lift, organize, or complete are good "talking time" materials. A child will be working a puzzle which he cannot complete, and another child will come along and offer his help. Conversation enters the picture. A girl is washing dishes in the house corner and needs a person to dry the dishes—talking takes place again. A boy needs help with a block building. Another child begins to help him. Through conversation each child learns of the other's ideas, suggestions, and abilities or inabilities.

SNACK TIME

This is a time for social language. The teacher can just listen for the trend of the conversation, for the interests of the children, and for the interaction of the group. If the teacher does not sit at the table with the children, the language will flow more freely. It will not be directed to her, as is so often the case when she is nearby.

ART

As a child works with the art media, there is a wonderful opportunity to converse and share ideas. "What is that you are making?" "How do you do that?" "Make me one, too" are entrances into the activities of others and another way to share language as well as abilities.

A child makes something with wood, clay, or other media, and has a wonderful story to tell about his finished product. The teacher encourages this, and may ask the children to ask the producer any questions about what he has made.

Recently an experiment was tried by the author using children in local schools. In cooperation with the teacher, the children in the kindergarten were asked to discuss what they knew about drums. During discussion many points were raised as to the drum's noise, it's shape, it's construction, it's material. Then the teacher said, "Let's have some fun and draw pictures of how *you* would act if you were a drum."

The resulting pictures were involved mostly with the idea that it wouldn't be much fun to be a drum because someone would be hitting you all the time, even in a parade which was fun to watch. But some children went in another direction in their interpretation. They depicted themselves as drums situated in a favorite occupation or setting. One boy drew his drum as a person sliding down a fireman's pole (Figure 10–1), and his story

FIGURE 10–1
Drum Sliding Down
Fireman's Pole

went like this: "I am a drum sliding down a fireman's pole. I feel like a fireman's drum because I like firehouses, and ride on the fire engines all the time."

GAMES

As the children are sitting together, the teacher may ask each of them to look around the room and find something *round*. Then they describe the round object, but do not give its name. The other children guess what the child has described.

Another game involves things the children bring to school. Place each item in an individual paper bag, or hide each object in the room. Have the child who has brought the object describe what he has brought. When the children guess from his description what the article is, the bag is opened to disclose the object.

Still another game that stimulates language, is a feel box or a paper bag. Place an item in either of these gadgets and have children feel and tell what is inside. In the case of the feel box, the children will reach in the box and touch the item with their hands. In the case of the paper bag, they will be feeling the outside of the bag and trying to guess from feeling the shape what the object might be.

DRAMATIZATION

The naturalness of children's actions, and the freedom with which speech can flow, makes dramatization another vehicle for language development. The child "plays" his favorite stories, acts out his role playing during free play, acts out his concerns and problems in order to understand them and relieve himself. All these actions bring about the use of words. He telephones on the toy telephone, and words he has heard at home are used fluently on the phone—sometimes with emphasis. The main interest of the teacher during these dramatizations is that the child develop a meaningful vocabulary and an ability to express himself. Whether or not he does an accurate dramatization of the story is not important.

PICTURES AND OBJECTS

Selection and display of interesting pictures will stimulate language among the children. One kindergarten boy saw a picture showing the bottom of the river with lobster pots, oysters, clams, and crabs. "What is that?" the boy wanted to know, as he touched the picture of the clam. "That is a clam," answered the teacher. "Would you like to see a real one tomorrow?"

When the boy agreed that he would like to see a clam, the teacher brought in one the next morning and opened it for the boy. This drew another child to the table to see what was on display, and the teacher stepped away from the group of children.

> Girl: What's that? Ugh!
>
> Boy: That's a clam. I saw it in a book and Mrs. G. got me one.
>
> Girl: What's that thing inside? It looks like a tongue.
>
> Boy (feeling the clam): It feels like a tongue. It's slippery.
>
> Girl: Can you pick it up?
>
> Boy (trying to lift the clam from the shell): No. It's stuck in the back.
>
> Girl: Let me touch it. (Lightly touches clam.) Oh, it's soft!
>
> Boy: Let's ask Mrs. G. what you can do with this.

Language was prompted by an object of interest to one child. It could easily have interested more children, but in this case only one other child was involved.

Many teachers choose pictures for the schoolroom because they are appealing to the teacher herself rather than to the children. When selecting a picture for children, find one which takes them beyond the familiar into the realm of the unfamiliar; for example, in choosing a snow scene, don't just find a picture of children sledding down a hill. Find a picture of mountain climbers scaling the snowy mountains; a picture of skiers speeding down the mountain side; a picture of toboggans whizzing down the raceway; or any other picture that says to the children, "This also happens in the snow."

Of course, artistry, size, the number of details, and the teacher's knowledge about what the group has experienced are important factors in selecting any picture for the classroom. Naturally, one of the teacher's aims is to cause children to look, question, and talk about the picture.

One teacher collected a group of pictures that showed different people at work—most of them outside the children's immediate environment. One showed men mining, one showed a dancing teacher with a class, one was of circus people in a relaxed situation (eating their dinners in the tent), one was a waiter in a hotel. The children were asked to look at these, and see if they would like to tell anything about any of the pictures. There was a response to every picture, and all the occupations were identified.

ANIMALS

Bringing an animal into the classroom as a pet, will cause much talking among children. The children's first questions and responses to the animal are the most interesting to tape or take down in shorthand. These are usually gleeful, exciting words with a sense of wonder in them found only in that first discovery, that first exposure. Watching the hatching of chickens is another experience that brings forth colorful language from the young child. It is also an opportunity for them to learn new words such as, "hatching," "thermometer," "pecking," and "scratching."

If no animals are in the classroom, another language experience is asking the children to talk about the kind of animal they would like to have if they could have one. The variety and types always astound the teacher, who usually thinks of dogs, cats, fish, guinea pigs, and rabbits. Children may express longing for otters, elephants, zebras, and other wild animals.

TRIPS

Taking children on excursions to nearby interesting places will add to the vocabulary of children. Not only will they add new words to their speech, but may clarify the meaning of both old and new vocabulary. Trips also have the added advantage of being real-life objects and people that had previously been encountered only in two dimensions in books and pictures. Now they become three-dimensional.

trip to upper school group

Visiting older children's rooms in school is always exciting for young boys and girls. Take them to see orchestra practice, ball games, gymnasium classes, or swimming teams. A visit to the home economics room in a high school is also good for getting children interested in cooking in nursery school and kindergarten. Language should be fluent after any of these visits.

visit to a library

It's nice to have the children look through and discuss books. It is good to hear the librarian read a story. However, children also can learn something about book care by watching repairs being made on torn books, covers being replaced, or marks being eradicated. Ask the librarian to show them some of these processes.

visit to a dairy

Visit one where the cows are a part of the business. In a large dairy children see milk going into bottles without any knowledge of how the milk gets into the machines for placement in the bottles. Let them touch the cows, see the cows milked, smell the odor of fresh milk, see it placed in large containers, and watch as it is delivered to the bottling section. These processes can be observed closely only in a small dairy, where the smallness makes it ideal. A small place is not so overwhelming to the young child as a large one and does not take so long to visit.

visit to a grocery store

Point out the storage and arrangement of the merchandise, but also let children observe how these supplies are delivered by trucks and how they are unloaded. An early morning visit would permit children to see this procedure.

At the grocery store, don't forget to watch the butcher cut the chops and steaks. If possible, follow up the trip by visiting a cannery or frozen food processing plant to give children a glimpse of how food is prepared before it is received by the stores.

visit to a veterinarian

Have the children look at the animals being cared for, but also have the doctor show them how the animals are bathed, given medicine, clipped, and so forth. Most children love to place their hands under the fluoroscope used by veterinarians and see their own bones. One child remarked after such an experience, "That's me? I look like Halloween."

TEACHER OBSERVATIONS

Young children's language can tell the teacher many things. She may notice mispronunciations that she will not correct, but rather she may use that mispronounced word several times in a story, a conversation, or during free play. She does this near the child who is having difficulty with the word and hopes he will hear the word pronounced correctly and will pick up the correct pronunciation.

A teacher may learn of children's misconceptions by listening.

> Boy (seeing a picture of a cow): That's a horse.
>
> Teacher: How do you know it's a horse?
>
> Boy: I just know.
>
> Teacher (showing him another picture of a horse): Do you know this animal?
>
> Boy: Yeh, that's a cow.

Here is a boy who needs to see a real cow and a real horse, so that he can compare and see the difference. A trip to a farm might solve this misconception.

READING STORIES

As the teacher is reading a story to the children, she stops in a strategic spot in the tale and asks the children what they think is going to happen. The children tell what could happen according to their reasoning or imaginations. This is the projecting of an event and is part of a reading background.

The teacher may read a poem which is not complete:

> I wish I were a pilot tall,
> I'd fly my plane over trees and _____.
> I'd go so high, a cloud I'd touch,
> I should like that very _____.

Children supply the words that they feel fit into the story. Some children will rhyme the words, some will not.

SUMMARY

There are many ways to provide children with opportunities to use language in the classroom. There are also opportunities for children to add new words and new concepts to their existing language, as they talk with their peers or with adults.

A teacher must remember that her own voice is not as important as the voices of children. She can control her impulse to talk all the time. Children cannot do this as easily. It is natural for each child to have so much to say that they just can't wait to let everyone, or someone, hear about it. When you have so much to tell the world, and you are so conscious of the fact that you can now express yourself with words, it is difficult to be quiet even when quiet is required.

11   the young child

his science experiences

The young child's natural curiosity leads him to investigate and examine each new thing he finds. He discovers rocks and he feels them, smells them, looks at them, and sometimes tastes them. He will also throw them, because this seems to be what rocks tell him to do.

He studies the windowpane as the rain beats against it, and is consumed with interest by the rivers of water that form as drops run together. He discovers flowers and immediately picks them, even when they are the neighbor's property.

Most of the child's concern is with his own immediate world. His glances do not necessarily go high into the air. It is the ground that seems to attract his attention. With this acute interest the child finds many things an adult will step over.

The "whys" of the young child are heard all during the school day, and the family is confronted with questions at home. When he sees something his curiosity is aroused and the questions flow forth. Because of this natural curiosity there is little need for the teacher to initiate an interest in his environment, science, or social studies. The interest, the curiosity, the exploratory desires are there for teachers to use as springboards to broader fields of learning.

This does not mean, however, that a nursery school or kindergarten teacher merely lets the natural curiosity of children go where it may.

There are various ways in which she can stimulate, foster, and develop the child's interest in the world in which he lives. To do so, she may find some or all of the following techniques and materials useful in her work with young children.

A "DO YOU KNOW" TABLE

A large table attractively covered, equipped with a magnifying glass and pictured nature books, and scaled to the child's eye level, may become an exploring place to which children are encouraged to bring objects from nature.

The teacher adds to the collection, a few things at a time, to encourage further observation and discussion. The following things may interest children:

1. various wild flowers,
2. a colony of ants,
3. unique plants not always seen in gardens or homes,
4. oysters in shells,
5. a praying mantis case,
6. a snake skin,
7. a silk worm,
8. tree bark,
9. pieces of coal.

The "do you know" table is a permanent fixture in the room, and changes character as the children and teacher bring in new additions. It holds insects, leaves, flowers, stones, small animals, magnets, water-measuring equipment, nuts, and any other thing that has aroused the interest of a child.

A LIBRARY

A teacher will admit freely that she often feels humble in the presence of young children, many of whom know a great deal about the fundamentals of science.

A prerequisite to understanding and liking science is an inquisitive mind. Children have this quality; the good teacher also must have a natural instinct for investigating and learning. The science books in the classroom should be selected for the teacher's information, as well as for the children's. For this reason, there should be a variety of reading materials ranging from the basic picture books to the more advanced scientific publications.

Lucky is the group whose teacher has retained an inquiring mind and a wonder about the world, and who is always searching for knowledge.

INTERESTS

It is often possible to draw more children into an undertaking by having them share their interests with others. The teacher tells the group about an activity in which a few children are participating, or the children involved explain to others what they are doing. For example, two children who are interested in planting some seeds might tell their classmates about their interest. By bringing this activity to the attention of other children, it is possible that a garden might be started by the group. If inside the classroom, the teacher might like to use wooden boxes, such as those in which large ginger ale bottles are sold. Each child could take one compartment of the box for his garden.

ACTIVITIES

A teacher who is aware of the interests of children and of the advantages of the school environment, can better suggest meaningful and interesting science activities. The following ideas can be of use in directing and encouraging children to discover more about the world around them.

science pictures

To help children become aware of their environment, and at the same time learn some of the names of things around them, take them on a nature walk. The object of the walk is to find things that may be glued or pasted on a piece of paper, wood, cardboard, or cloth.

If the teacher has a large table ready in the schoolroom, the children can place the findings in containers on the table—twigs in one container, leaves in another, buds in another, flowers in another, pebbles in another, acorns in another.

Nearby, the teacher could place glue, tape, string, staplers, small wooden boxes, cardboard tubes from paper products, and any other things that might be used with the discovered materials. This array gives children a choice of materials, a choice of applicator, and a chance to do some problem solving. A large science picture is the result.

leaves

Encourage children to notice the changing colors of leaves and to bring different leaves to school. Have the children separate the leaves by color, size, or shape. This gives children a chance to notice differences in leaves and to categorize them.

Make a tree in the room by covering a large can with a mixture of fine sawdust and wheat paste, mixed with water. This makes a trunk for the tree. Fill the container with dirt and insert a large twig inside the can. Have the children paste leaves or berries on the twig. The appearance of the tree can change with the changing of the seasons, helping the children to observe and note changes.

Have the children play a game using leaves or flowers. Place these on a board and have children find mates for them. These are the likenesses and differences that are a background for mathematics and reading.

Have a treasure hunt. Ask children to find the largest leaf on the playground. They can also find the smallest leaf, various kinds of ferns, different kinds of seeds, or different barks. A child's understanding of variations in materials is strengthened in this way.

plants

Transplant and pot some plants for the children to care for indoors. Plant in narrow glass bowls so the roots may be observed, and children can become aware of the various parts of plants and the functions of these parts.

galls

Look for large swellings on oak trees (galls). Help the children to cut these open and see where tiny larvae live. Cook the galls in a little water and make brown paint. Children will see that paint can be homemade and that the fun of making it is gratifying.

sounds

Take a walk and listen for sounds. Have the children tell what they heard after they return from the walk. This causes children to be alert to things around them and to use their senses to find out about things. It also gives them opportunity to reproduce sounds and enjoy a guessing game with the other children.

Fill glass bottles with colored water—each bottle with a different level of water. Suspend these from a broom handle with a heavy cord on each. Have the children strike the bottles with a wooden mallet and listen for the different sounds each makes. It is possible to make a scale this way. If the bottles are sealed tightly, the water will not evaporate as quickly.

rest

Take an outdoor rest. While the children are on their backs, have them look into the sky for cloud formations. Play a game, "I see a _____." The children are using their imaginations in a constructive manner, as well as verbalizing their thoughts.

EQUIPMENT

What better way to stimulate investigation than by having materials on hand for children to try and to observe:

1. magnets,
2. compass,
3. thermometer,
4. prism,
5. ruler or tape,
6. weighing machine,
7. inclined plane,
8. pulley.

Children will be interested not only in looking at these, but in seeing what they can do. Encourage them to try things over and over. Encourage the use of the thermometer by adding a pan of ice and a pan of warm water to the table. Hang the prism in a sunny window, but low enough for children to observe the colors. Place small blocks or weights near the scales so children can balance objects. By the inclined plane place a small automobile that can roll down the plane. Near the magnets place objects that can and cannot be attracted.

TEACHER-MADE SCIENCE MATERIALS

Science activities are important to children, not only for science's sake, but for the language development, arithmetic background, and the opportunity for the child to learn about his world.

In nursery school and kindergarten, children should be encouraged to find out about their world through looking, listening, feeling, and smelling. It is through this awakening of the senses that the child's world can be broadened and deepened.

To encourage this learning, the teacher may make different pieces of equipment for the room to encourage children to bring in animals, plants, and inanimate objects for classroom display and observation. Here are some ideas.

container for small insects

Use a can opener to remove the bottom from a coffee can, candy tin, or small cake tin. Cut screening into a circle to fit the bottom of the can. Secure the screening to the can with mystic tape (Figure 11–1).

Paint the lid and the can to prevent rusting. (Avoid using green, which makes the can difficult to see in the grass.) Paint the interior of the can

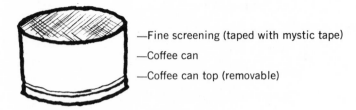

—Fine screening (taped with mystic tape)

—Coffee can

—Coffee can top (removable)

FIGURE 11–1   Small Insect Container

some light color to facilitate seeing insects in action (cream, yellow, or white work well). Place the lid on the other side of the can.

This can may be placed on its side with the screen side out, so that children may see the insects easily. The device is extremely useful to take on a walk for bringing home animals and insects which children find.

insectarium (for flies, ants, butterflies, and moths)

Fill a clay pot with good loose dirt. Place a glass chimney in the dirt with some plant life inside the chimney. Cover the top of the chimney with a plastic dish cover that has fine holes punched in it (Figure 11–2). Keep the plant life moist by sprinkling it with water. Insects may be seen clearly through the glass.

cocoon holder

To permit children to watch a moth or butterfly emerge in its own habitat, make a cocoon or chrysalis holder (Figure 11–3). Fold hardware cloth into the shape of a bag and tape the rough edges with mystic tape. Sew or tape a piece of cotton material to the open end of the wire. Place a draw-string through the end of the cloth. Place the bag over a tree limb on which a cocoon or chrysalis is attached, and draw the string tightly. In

FIGURE 11–2
Insectarium

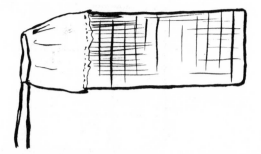

FIGURE 11–3
Cocoon Holder

this way, children may watch the day-to-day development of the cocoon without forcing the insect out of its home ahead of season, as it would be if the cocoon were kept indoors.

container for praying mantis

Remove the top from a coffee tin, candy tin, or cake tin. Place a roll of fine wire, taped together at the seams and a foot high, inside the can. Replace the container's top on the top of the wire (Figure 11–4). A small branch set inside the container gives the mantis a place on which to sit

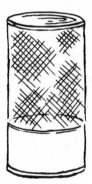

FIGURE 11–4
Praying Mantis
Container

or on which to deposit a case. The same kind of container may be used to observe a caterpillar spin a cocoon. By reading a story about the needs of a caterpillar, the teacher may inspire the children to bring in insects for the caterpillar to eat.

terrarium number one

Tape four pieces of glass together with colored mystic tape to form a box-shaped piece (Figure 11–5). Front and back panes should measure thirteen inches in length; sides should measure nine and one-half inches. All pieces should be about nine inches high.

Mix plaster of Paris and pour it into a shallow cookie tray. Place the glass structure in the tray before the plaster of Paris hardens. A fifth piece

FIGURE 11–5
Terrarium Number One

of glass, thirteen inches long and nine and one-half inches wide, forms the top. Tape the edges of the top with mystic tape. On the inside of the terrarium place a layer of pebbles for drainage, then a layer of dead leaves, then soil and moss.

This terrarium may also be used as a vivarium for newts, salamanders, and frogs if the top is opened slightly to allow air to enter.

Water on the leaves of the plants will give the amphibians drinking water. A small pan filled with water and inserted in the dirt will give the animals opportunity to wet their skins.

terrarium number two

A less expensive terrarium may be made by cleaning out a gallon jug (Figure 11–6). Place charcoal in the bottom of the jar to help keep the soil

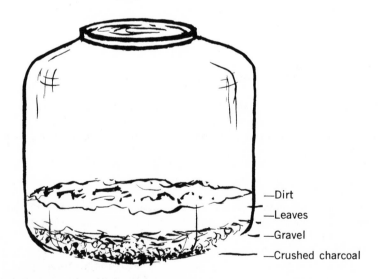

FIGURE 11–6   Terrarium Number Two

sweet. Put about one inch of gravel on top of the charcoal for drainage. Then add one layer of leaves and one of dirt. Use a good deal of moss, and add about four plants. Be sure the roots of the plants are pushed into the soil. Place a lid on the jar.

Keep the terrarium lightly watered. Lack of condensation on the top will indicate when water is needed.

This same jar may be used as a vivarium by replacing the lid with a piece of small screen covering the opening of the bottle, or by cutting out a circle on the top of the lid and taping in the wire, or by punching small holes in a plastic dish cover.

The jar may be placed on its side in a cigar box. Cut a semicircle in the box to fit the neck of the jar in order to prevent the jar from rolling.

rabbit hutch

Find two apple crates. Remove an end from one of the crates. Cut a round hole in the other end, large enough for the animal to crawl through (Figure 11–7). After insulating the box with corrugated cardboard, replace

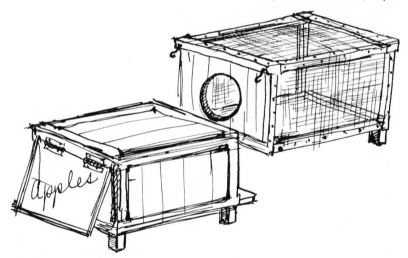

FIGURE 11–7   Rabbit Hutch

the end that was removed, using hinges and hooks (to allow for easy cleaning). Cover the top.

Make a framework from the other crate by cutting out all sides except one. (Leave enough wood in the corners of the crate to hold wire.) In the remaining side make a hole corresponding in size and position to the one in the first crate. Nail wire over the top, bottom, two sides, and one end of the second crate.

Put legs on the front of the wire crate and on both ends of the other crate. Place a small ledge on one end of the fully enclosed crate, large enough for the wire box to rest on. Put hooks on the back end of the wire box and corresponding hook eyes on the front of the other crate. Paint all woodwork. Hook the two crates together.

This type of rabbit hutch gives the animals an open air place, as well as a hiding place.

cage with treadle

Saw wood into sections to make five picture frames, two twelve by twelve inch sections, and three nineteen by twelve inch sections. Four of these frames form the sides of the cage; the fifth is the top. Staple quarter inch wire mesh onto the frames. Then nail the frames into the shape of the cage (Figure 11–8). Staple wire mesh across the bottom. (Wire mesh should cover the wooden frame inside to prevent the animal from gnawing the wood.)

An exercise treadle may be made by bending wire mesh into the size of

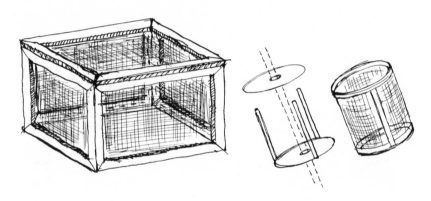

FIGURE 11–8   Cage with Treadle

circle desired. Tape the edges to protect the animal. Cut four two inch tin circles from the tops of coffee cans. Cut six lengths from coat hangers. Solder three of the wires to the tin circle, then place another tin circle on top and solder it securely. (Repeat for other side.) Solder the tops of the wires to the mesh circles. Put a rod through the holes in the tin circles, making sure the tread will turn easily.

flower holder

Wire small medicine bottles onto a pegboard, and fill the bottles with water. These bottles serve as containers for various kinds of flowers, or for seeds which the children find and bring to school. Instead of placing all the flowers in one vase, and having the children's contribution lost in the large bunch, individual attention is given to each donation by placing the flowers in separate containers.

SUMMARY

Science activities are important to children not only for science's sake. Through science experiences, language develops, arithmetic evolves, reading occurs (if only in picture form), and the child learns more about the world in which he lives.

Perhaps children are interested in trains. They visit a station. While there, they learn how trains are used by people and how trains travel, but also they learn that electricity or sometimes steam, makes the train travel. This is learning, both in social studies and in science. Where does one begin and the other end?

A class visits a post office. The children see not only what happens to their letters and where the mail for their homes is sorted, but also the machinery that stamps the letters, the conveyor belt that transports heavy packages, and the trucks that carry heavy loads of mail. Science is here, too.

The aim of science in nursery school and kindergarten is to encourage children to find out about their world through looking, listening, feeling, and smelling. It is through this awakening of the senses that the child's world broadens and deepens.

12   the young child

his mathematics

The nursery school or kindergarten child has been exposed to mathematical experiences in his home life. There, and elsewhere, the child has witnessed various shapes through his own observation, and through adults pointing out difference in sizes and shapes of toys and other materials. He has thought, evaluated, and verbalized with such comments as, "Your ice cream cone is larger than mine"; "I want two of those"; "I will give you one of these for two of those."

In addition to experiencing differences in size and shape, the child has also had experiences in placing things in space. Such comments as, "I will drive the wagon down this way and put it over there," is one evidence of this space experience. He is visualizing himself in the space in which he finds himself and is able to move his body, or a machine, through this space.

He has experiences in accumulating objects around the house and in the yard, and thereby makes these objects into one large amount. He is learning that things or people may be placed in like groups. He most probably is a rote counter who sings or chants the numbers, without understanding the concept of what makes up that number. The nursery school and kindergarten teacher exposes the young child to mathematics in many forms. This is not formalized instruction, but rather an offering of activities to bring about mathematical learnings.

COUNTING

So often children count by rote. To *prevent* this, they should touch objects as they count them. These objects are placed a few spaces apart so the child sees them as separate pieces and not as a whole.

attendance

The teacher may take attendance by asking the children to count with her as she touches each child. As the child is touched, he sits down. This gives children a concept of parts making up the whole set or collection. It also shows them that counting is done by counting *something* and not just by saying the numbers. Touching the children tells each of them that he has been counted, and should sit down. Touching each child also slows down the counting of the children, because they wait until a child is touched before they say the number.

The teacher could make a paper doll picture of each child, and then place these on a wall or board. When a child is absent their picture is turned upside down. Then, together, the teacher and children count the upright pictures as the teacher points to each doll. "Don't count until I touch the doll," she may say to the children if they are counting ahead of her.

The teacher can use a flannel board, and as each child enters the school he places a form of some kind on the board, placing them from left to right, and in rows of ten. (Having squares marked on the board, on which to place the forms, is a guide for the children.) The second row is lined up with the first row (as are the third row, the fourth row, etc.) so that forms are in line with the preceding row. By grouping in tens the children may get the concept of counting the first row as ten, and then counting the other forms by ones.

play centers

When an activity permits just so many children to work in an area at one time, the child will have to count to see if there is available space for him in that activity. Does he make too many? Does he make just enough? This gives a child a feeling of responsibility for his own actions in selecting his work or play, in addition to giving him counting practice.

calendar

Sometimes when an important day or event is in the offing, the teacher and children may count the days on a large calendar to see how many more days there are before the event occurs. The important date is marked with some symbol to limit the count at that point.

serving

Children do counting as they serve at snack time. It may be counting the milk for each table, counting the cookies or crackers for the table, or counting the napkins or place settings for the table. Sometimes it is a matter of counting out special "goodies" brought in by some child, and each member of the group is to receive a predetermined amount of the treat.

materials

If crayons are kept in their box, children may check after using the crayons to ascertain if the correct number are returned to the box. This is to make sure that the next person to use the box will have all the crayons belonging in that box. The same rule could also apply to puzzle pieces.

stories

There are many stories that involve counting. Children can follow as the teacher reads the numbers, points to the objects in the book, and has everyone count them.

music, games, finger plays

Activities often include songs, games, and finger plays that involve the use of cardinal or ordinal numbers. (See chapter 14 for finger plays involving the use of mathematics.)

WORKBENCH

Arithmetic often is needed at a workbench. The child measures, if not with a measuring tape or stick, then by placing wood pieces together and comparing sizes. He experiences thickness, width, and length. His conversation contains such terms as: "long enough," "too short," and "about the same."

Further arithmetic is sponsored by having a storage space for all the tools. A board is placed near the workbench, (a bulletin board may be used) and an outline of the tools is drawn on this holder. This gives children a spot to place their implements. After comparing shapes and sizes he arranges them in their proper places on the board. He does this by following the direction of the form and, thereby, placing the handle or head in the right spot. Here is an opportunity for the child to compare likenesses and differences.

WATER PLAY

If children are given the proper materials—a water table, plastic bottles, plastic cups, strainers, ladles, and other equipment—they will begin to measure. Some child fills a small cup with water and, by pouring it in a bottle, finds that it takes two cups to fill the bottle with water. The child takes the same cup and fills a larger container. He sees that it takes more cups for this container than it did for the bottle. He is becoming conscious of size difference and content difference.

The child pours water into various shapes of containers, and finds that water takes the shape of the object into which it is poured. So, water can have a round shape, a square shape, an oval shape, or a rectangular shape. Without the container it would have no specific shape, but rather would run and spread. Here is mathematics and science in one experience.

COOKING

Adding pictured recipe books to the house corner may prompt dramatic play, but it may also inspire children to try real cooking. The boys and girls could make their own dough, using pictures of the correct quantities of each ingredient. This involves the children in measuring.

Once cookies are made, the class could have a bake sale at which each child could sell cookies to his own parents. Again, the children would have a chance to experience counting—if the cookies sold for one penny each, and each parent was limited to purchasing no more than five. Money and its value are important in mathematics. Money made in this way could be used to buy something special for the room, which the children could select, based on the amount of money they have on hand.

GARDENING

To introduce mathematics into a garden project, have each child measure the boundaries for his individual garden, using a wooden ruler. If each line were one foot, a foot ruler would not require difficult measuring. This would involve each child in using a ruler, and marking off the spot as it is measured. It also offers the child a responsibility for the planting and care of his own garden.

BLOCKS

Using blocks offers children many mathematical experiences. Here are just a few of them.

terms

With blocks the child begins using mathematical terms such as, "too long," "too wide," "not enough," "two more," and many other terms. These words begin to flow as the child experiments with the blocks—trying to make them equal to each other, trying to cover a necessary break in a building, trying to balance blocks one upon the other, trying to make extensions on buildings that will not make the building fall.

spatial concepts

As a child uses blocks, he is working in space—fitting his structure into a place in space that must have adequate length, width, and height. As his blocks come in contact with the room wall, he realizes that his building must go in another direction if he wants to enlarge it or add to it.

shapes

Blocks also offer children the experience of shapes that are different but that can be fitted together to make a larger shape. Here he is beginning to see likenesses and differences in form, as well as the way forms can be fitted together without having excess length, width, or height in the wrong places.

equivalency

As the child works with blocks, he is finding that a certain number of blocks are required to equal the length or width of another block. So, he places six blocks perpendicular to a single block to equal the length of the long block. He is really measuring the long block.

fractions

As children handle blocks they are sometimes working with fractional parts of a whole. The half-circle blocks make a complete circle when two are fitted together; the quarter-circle blocks make a complete circle when four are fitted together; two triangular blocks become a diamond-shaped form or a larger triangle. There are many other small parts which make a whole when the pieces are placed together.

TRIPS

A trip planned by the school might involve the child's use of money. He is responsible for bringing ten cents to school, which is to be used for the purchase of peanuts for the elephants at the zoo. At the zoo the child purchases his own bag of nuts. This may be his first exposure to buying.

SUMMARY

Mathematics are going on in the nursery school and kindergarten as the children play with blocks, work at the workbench, fit puzzles together, distribute snacks and other items, use finger plays, play games, and listen to stories that involve numbers. These activities present to the child the parts that make up the whole, the counting with cardinal and ordinal numbers, the shapes and sizes of various materials and how these sizes and shapes differ and are alike.

The teacher takes advantage of opportunities, as they arise in the schoolroom, to aid the children in their understanding of mathematical terms and values. There is categorizing by selecting things which are alike and placing them together. A child learns first the value of numbers, then he begins to pick them out or write them. This gives him an understanding of what the numeral stands for before he learns to read or write that numeral.

13   the young child

his social studies

Part of the social studies to which children are exposed in nursery school and kindergarten is the group living that occurs in all parts of the program. This may be the child's first contact with children his own age, and there must be an adjustment in his thinking, actions, and feelings about himself and others.

At home the young child may have had the whole house revolving around him. In the school situation he must learn that all his wants and needs are not fulfilled; others have to be considered, too. He must learn to live and work with people he has not known before entering the school. It is the teacher's job to see that each child is given dignity, that each child adjusts to the new situation with understanding and happiness. She does this mostly through example—by accepting each child for his own uniqueness, by helping each child feel that what he contributes to the class is important, and by utilizing the capabilities of each child.

IN THE SCHOOL

There is contact in the school with individual children as the child works and plays with first one and then another child. Through language, parallel play, cooperative play, and the sharing of personal possessions and school materials, children come in contact with other children. They learn many things through this contact—that people do not all think alike, do not all act alike, have different ideas, and can help you if you need help.

The teacher makes sure there are opportunities for individual play, for small group play, and for the entire group to come together to share a story, a snack, or a trip. Most of her group members have had opportunities at home to play in community groups. Here in nursery school and kindergarten, they have an opportunity to socialize with others—with the teacher's guidance offering positive or negative reinforcement.

As the child learns about others' needs, social activities, drives, and backgrounds, he is also learning about himself. He learns that he cannot always do things the way he wants to do them, even if that has been the case away from school. He learns that there are ways to approach others, and that a verbal approach is more acceptable than a push or hit. He learns that everything is not his, that things now belong to everyone, and that he must learn to share and take his turn. He learns that he has a responsibility to other children. He is just one of this group who must put things in their places so all the children will be able to find them. He learns to care for play materials because everyone in the group wants them kept in good shape. A car with broken wheels, a doll without a head, or a puzzle with a missing piece do not make interesting and enticing toys.

The child is given the responsibility of caring for his own things. In a special spot or cubby assigned to him, he places clothing, papers, and "treasures" brought from home. He learns to respect the privacy of others, to put belongings only in his own cubby, and to take things out of only his own place.

OUTSIDE THE SCHOOL

In addition to socializing with the school community, the child is also given experience with the community outside the schoolroom.

The teacher brings the children into contact with the outer environment by taking children on trips and bringing community people into the classroom. She takes advantage of a worker who comes to the school, or near it—a telephone man, a furnace man, a painter, a policeman assigned to the school area, a milkman, a repair man, and any other worker who visits the school.

The teacher takes the children to visit these people. By seeing and observing them, the child learns about the many persons who are a part of this life in the community. Teachers should stress the value of these workers as their work applies to the child. What can this worker do for you? What does this worker give you? Let's try the opposite approach as well. What can *we* do for these workers? What can *we* do to help these people do a better job?

IDEAS FOR SOCIAL ACTIVITIES

1. Make gifts for a children's hospital, such as gifts for food trays, or books containing children's paintings or drawings. Maybe a story written by the children would please the patients.

2. Have a child's father visit the school and tell about the work he does. If he has any props for his business or trade, have him bring these when he calls. Imagine the joy of the children if a father were to bring his tools and make a piece of equipment for the school! The children could join in and help with the production.

3. The children could plan a special entertainment for visitors who are coming to see the school. A teacher too often considers a visitor *her* company. Let the children plan where the visitors can sit, what the children can do to make them comfortable, and what they would like to be doing when the visitors are there.

4. If a parent has a new baby, take the children to her home and let her show them how she feeds and bathes the baby.

5. Have a fireman bring his fire truck to the school. Away from the bustle and surprise calls at the fire house, the children can sit on the truck, ring the bell, try on the hat and, naturally, ask questions.

6. Go to a post office and take letters for each child to mail. These letters could be prepared by children (in picture form) and sent as Valentines, holiday greetings, or surprises for Mother and Dad. Watch the letters being stamped at the post office counter, watch the filing of letters by areas, and ask to see mail box allotments belonging to the streets on which the children live.

7. Visit a garage where children can see men working on cars. It's nice to do this when the school bus is in the shop for repairs.

8. If the insurance permits, ask a baking company if the children can visit to watch bread or cookies being made. Be sure it is a small bakery and that the mixing vats, etc., are within eye range of the child. Children can follow this up by baking in the classroom.

9. A local florist could be interesting for young children. Have him arrange a bouquet and show the children some planting of seeds or seedlings. This may be followed by the children starting their own gardens with seeds or plants obtained at the florist's.

10. A small exhibit of paintings, within the children's interest and understanding, sometimes brings out interesting observations on the part of the children. Why does the person make the whole picture with blue paint? Why does the artist show yellow lines in the sky? One school, after such a visit, had their own art show which was composed of paintings by members of the kindergarten.

11. Go to a high school and watch a baton twirler practicing. Watch the band march and play instruments.

12. If there is a rug weaver, a basket weaver, and a china painter in the neighborhood, have the children visit them.

13. A tailor shop may be visited where children can see people making clothes. A children's shop is even better.

14. Have a mother come to school and make a special cake while the children watch. A gingerbread house or gingerbread men are great to watch and the children can participate in the decorating.

15. Show some simple films of children planting gardens, or children in other lands doing things that children in this country do.

16. Take children to watch a shoemaker mend a shoe. The teacher could take a pair of her own shoes.

17. Watch an artist paint a simple picture. If possible, have him tell a story as he paints.

18. Ask any parents who play musical instruments to bring their instruments and accompany the children as they sing. Children could also use the school instruments to play along with the parents.

19. Have a trainer bring his dog to class and watch as the dog goes through obedience training tactics.

20. Have an upper-grade class give a puppet show. This could inspire the children to make puppets or to use the puppets in their room.

21. Ask a football player to come to school and play ball with the children.

22. Have some of the older children in the school do a dance for the group. Maybe the older children could teach a simple dance to the nursery school or kindergarten children.

SUMMARY

The social studies program in nursery school and kindergarten is two-fold. One aspect is the social adjustment of the child in a school setting, in which he learns about himself and others. The other part of his social studies brings him into contact with the community. He observes people and things that aid him. At the same time, he may learn what he can do to aid these community workers.

14   the young child

his games

The word "game" becomes a part of the child's vocabulary at a very early age. While he is an infant, his family will play "hide and seek", finger and toe games, eating games to entice appetites, going-to-bed games that hurry the child to sleep, and going-in-the-car games that help pass away long trips for the restless child and calm adult's nerves. These are usually games that the adult has improvised to gain the child's attention, to help him pass time, or to help him forget some difficult thing.

The game may be a truly physical experience; for example, the adult tosses the child into the air and then catches him. This may be the infant's first contact with space, where his body is not touching some person or object. The games may be make-believe ones in which adult and child pretend or fantasize through the activity of a game.

As soon as he is able to walk or crawl, the young child will begin to improvise games of his own. He may crawl to a shelf of books and take them down and pile them on the floor. He will empty drawers and place their contents in a container or in a pile. This is his way of investigating his world and, at the same time, playing games with the materials in his environment. Sometimes these materials are more appealing to him than his own toys.

When the child can walk and speak, his games take on a different aspect. He still improvises, but adds more detail to what he is doing. The 3- and

4-year-old will make up a game on the spur of the moment. "Let's pretend that I run over there, and you chase me!" "I'll do this and then you do it!" "I'll jump over this stone and you do it!" "You do everything I do!" These are games which do not last too long, and often change character after just a few minutes. The children may be running and touching the fence, and after a few runs the organizer or some other child might say, "I know what! Let's hit the fence with a stone and then fall down." Sometimes, these changes are suggested during a game because the child who is suggesting them is not doing too well in the original game.

Young children enjoy vigorous games and, therefore, their outdoor games seem most enjoyed by them. These games involve running, jumping, pulling, and any other bodily exercise that uses a great deal of energy. Children seem to participate least in games where there has to be a winner, or where someone is singled out as doing something wrong. It would be of interest for someone to study organized games as compared to simple sense games to discover which of these is of the most interest to young children, and which has the most participants.

Playing games in preschool groups was introduced in the Froebelian kindergartens in Germany, about the middle of the nineteenth century. From that time until around the 1930s, games continued as a vital part of every kindergarten program, and also appeared in nursery schools.

These early games based on the Froebelian philosophy of education, were highly organized, contained many directions for the children to follow, and were often competitive. Many games were about something the children did not understand or know about. Such games as "Dame Get Up and Bake Your Pies," "Sally Go Round the Stars," and other games with words that meant nothing to the children, were used daily in many preschool groups. The games were selected by the teacher without offering children a chance to choose a game they might like to play. They were also completely teacher-directed, often with the teacher telling children when it was their turn to move, jump, run, or talk.

In contrast to those early days, today's games mostly involve the use of the senses. Because children learn much from the use of hands, eyes, ears, and mouth, preschool teachers take advantage of this knowledge by helping children become aware of word meanings, spatial concepts, color awareness, and social learnings.

Games are not often competitive because teachers realize that a child of this age cannot understand competition. Games also contain only about two or three directions. The children can easily remember the sequence, which could be more difficult to recall if there were too many directions.

Games often stress color, shape, quantitative concepts, imitations of actions set by one individual, listening for sounds for identification or reproduction, or physical activity. Other games may be used for speech articulation, visual acuity, identification through touch, mental alertness, and taste discrimination. The teacher presents games with certain aims in mind to aid the children in understandings or learnings.

The teacher, however, does not overlook the fact that games are just plain fun. Say to any adult or child, "How about playing a game?" and agreement is usually forthcoming. We never outgrow our love of having fun.

TYPES OF GAMES

Games may be categorized to determine their value for children. Are they physical games, concept games, imitation games, speech games, tactile games, sense games, or just plain fun games? What is being stressed as the game is introduced?

stressing color and shape

Game 1.   Color small boxes with paper, paint, or crayons. Use vivid, true colors, primary or secondary. The children should be familiar with the colors used. Many young children know not only the basic colors but also tints and shades.

Use poker chips or make cardboard circles using the same colors that appear on the boxes.

The object of the game is to place the circle in the box whose color matches it. After all the circles are in place, they may be counted to verify that each box has the same number of circles. This is the child's verification of the problem. He is checking his own correctness.

Game 2.   Another game, which can be made by the teacher, involves making a large cardboard triangle, a large square, and a large circle. These are placed in the middle of a table. Children are given small forms which correspond to the shapes on the table.

As the teacher calls the name of a form, the children place the small forms on the larger corresponding forms. There are enough shapes of each kind so that several children can place their small triangles, circles, or squares on the larger shapes simultaneously.

This same game can be made more difficult by having two large forms of each shape on the table, and having each set in different colors (two triangles—one red and one blue; two circles—one green and one black; or two squares—one brown and one yellow). When the shape is called, the color is also named, and then the child places the right color and shape in the appropriate place. This gives the children more of a problem-solving approach because two things must be looked for and decided upon.

Game 3.   For another color game, place a colored card on a child's back. See if another child can see the color and name it. The child with the color attached to his back, by the use of a safety pin or string holding it around his neck, must turn and dodge the other child so that his color may not be seen.

Game 4.   Pass out various shapes or colors to children. These are pinned on the front or back of the child. Then the children try to find their mate by going from one child to another, until they find the form or color that matches theirs.

stressing quantitative concept

Game 1.   Children sit in a circle. Each child is given three or four colored objects or papers. A tablecloth is placed in the middle of the circle which becomes a garden.

The teacher says, "Please plant all the yellow flowers in our garden; please plant all the red flowers in our garden, etc." As each color is named, the children place their paper (or a flower may be made of paper) on the cloth.

This may also be played by the teacher saying, "All the boys who have yellow flowers, please plant them; all the girls who have yellow flowers, please plant them." If a child has difficulty recognizing a color, the teacher may want to give him that color to help him recognize it. This game may also be played by using a flannel board, instead of a cloth, for a garden.

Game 2.   Using ten children, play the following game by enacting this poem:

> Ten little mice looking for cheese,
> They run on the floor as nice as you please.
> Ten little mice climb up high,
> They eat and eat a great big pie.
> Ten big cats out looking for fun,
> They chase the mice and make them run.

This is a running and catching game that requires twenty children to enact.

stressing imitation and identification

Game 1.   When children are in a group, ask one child to make a sound he hears around his home. The other children identify the sound.

It may be a good idea to have the performing child whisper in the teacher's ear what he is going to do. A child who wants to have a longer turn may change his mind when the children have guessed correctly, and he may tell them they are wrong so his turn will continue. In the meantime, he will be thinking of some substitute for his original idea.

Game 2.   A sound box is another way for children to identify sounds with which they are familiar. The box should be deep, and placed higher than the children's heads.

Inside the box the teacher places such items as: egg beater, bell, small drum, two glasses (one containing water which is poured from one glass to another), a small whisk broom (to represent the sound of a large broom), an alarm clock, spoons, etc. These objects are hit, turned, poured, or run and children guess what the object is.

stressing physical activity

Game 1.   Large circles (about two yards in diameter) are placed around the playground. Three or four children are stationed on each circle.

At a given signal, the children run from one circle to the other. At the next signal, everyone stops on any circle.

Game 2.   Skip tag is a highly physical game. One child starts skipping as the music is played. He, in turn, tags some other child who joins him in skipping. The second child tags another child, and the game goes on like this until everyone is skipping.

Some children may say, "I can't skip," so it might be a good idea not to call it a skipping game. If the music is played and it is a skipping rhythm, children forget they are supposed to skip and usually do it unconsciously in response to the music.

stressing speech

Young children often have difficulty with certain sounds at the beginning of words, or in the middle of words. They may substitute sounds or omit them. This is characteristic, and does not necessarily mean that remedial steps are necessary at this early age. However, games may be used to strengthen or perhaps correct language.

Game 1.   Take a simple song like *Jingle Bells.* Children usually like to sing this song all during the year. If the song is requested off-season, the teacher may suggest that the children play a game, using this song.

"Children, let's pretend we have some bells here on the floor in front of us. Pick up this big one over here. Do you know what it says? It says "s-s-s-s." Let's have the bell sing *Jingle Bells* with its s-s-s-s sound!"

The children sing the tune using the "s" sound throughout the song. Try other sounds children have difficulties in pronouncing. "r" (sometimes pronounced like "w") and "th" (sometimes pronounced like "v") are common mispronunciations.

Game 2.   Another fun game is to have each child say something in a tape recorder. This is done privately, so no one but the teacher will hear him taping. Then, use this tape and have children listen and identify the person who is talking. Put in *your* voice, too!

stressing visual acuity

Game 1.   Place four or five objects on a table. The children identify them before starting the game, so the object will have a common name for all to use. Cover the objects with a cloth, and have children name what they have seen. Change the objects or their positions.

Take this game a step further by naming the objects, then, taking some object away and having the children name the missing object. Change the position of objects after taking one out of the group, as children may remember spaces where objects are located. This makes it a little more difficult.

Game 2. Another visual game, which could be used for visual acuity, is having one child describe another child in the group. Then have the children guess the identity of the described person.

Game 3. Try this game at Christmas time. Children often bring Christmas toys to school. If enough of these are in the room, the teacher could have them placed on a table along with some of the school toys. Each child describes the present he received, and the rest of the children try to identify it by going to the table and pointing it out.

Game 4. Ask the children to look around the room and find everything that is a "circle," "square," and a "triangle."

stressing tactile discrimination

Game 1. Select objects that children know, and place each object in a paper bag. Close each bag with a rubber band, and pass the bag around the group. The children feel the bag and then name what is inside it.

This can be done with fruits, vegetables, toys, wooden animals, or any other room object which will fit into a small bag. Be sure the objects have distinctive features.

This game may also be used when children bring in their "treasures" from home. The bag becomes a surprise bag. Children again feel the outside of the container, and try and guess what is inside. Everyone who wants to do so will guess before the bag is opened and the object shown.

Game 2. Obtain a large wooden box, or a sturdy cardboard box. Cut a round hole in the front, and attach the sleeve lining from a coat in the hole. The top or side of the box is fitted with a hinge or hook, so that things may be placed inside the "feel box."

Alongside the box, place a large piece of paper with drawings or pictures of various objects—one of which is identical to the object in the box. After children feel inside the box, they choose a picture which they feel is identical to the article in the box.

stressing quiet

Game 1. Try a game where no one talks. This is good after an especially boisterous time, and tends to help children relax.

Take a large piece of oilcloth or heavy plastic, and mark off into large squares. In each square place a picture. These pictures are not complete, but the children hold the missing parts—it may be an airplane with a wing missing, a boy without a shoe, or a tree without a trunk.

Starting with a child, ask him to find the place where his picture goes. Then continue around the circle until all the pictures are completed. Going in a circle lets children know that their turn will be after the child's next to him. This may avoid the children frantically asking for a turn.

Game 2.   Have a list of true and false statements within the children's experience background. Have children raise arms when the statement is true, and put their hands in their laps when the statement is false. Any kind of movement can be used for the quiet response.

stressing mental alertness

Game 1.   Use the old favorite *Hickory-Dickory-Dock.* Decide what time the clock is going to strike. As the children sing the song, have them substitute the chosen time in place of the usual "one."

Ask children to clap each time a number is sung—five claps for each count of five o'clock, etc. This gives them a concept of each number and a knowledge of how many numbers a clock can strike. It's fun if a play clock is set each time a number is suggested.

Game 2.   Go on a listening walk. When children return to their schoolroom, have them take turns repeating a sound they heard on the walk, or describing something they saw. The other children guess what the sound or description is.

Game 3.   Give each child three things to do. For example, ask a child to "stand up; go to the window; and then come back and shake my hand."

Children, in order to do this, must remember the sequence of the request. With some children, who are less mature, two commissions are enough at a time.

Game 4.   Use the game:

> I'm very, very tall,
> I'm very, very small.
> Sometimes tall,
> Sometimes small,
> Guess what I am now?

This is usually done as a game in which one child closes his eyes, and guesses whether the children are tall or small, as the last line indicates.

Take this same song and change it, using any of the following ideas to point out contrasts:

> I'm very, very fat; I'm very, very thin, or
> I'm very, very happy; I'm very, very sad, or
> I'm very, very mad; I'm very, very glad, or
> I'm very, very stiff; I'm very, very limp.

Children express the words by motions or facial expressions as the words are sung.

stressing taste discrimination

Game 1.   Ask each child, in turn, to close his eyes and taste a small piece of a familiar food. Watch them miss many foods they eat daily!

TEACHER-MADE GAMES

There is always satisfaction in making up and creating your own games. In doing this the teacher can have exactly the right game for her group, plus the correct size for her room. She may even decide to make the material a folding type if her room is too small for much equipment.

interest center

Pictured here (Figure 14–1) is a play material that offers opportunity for many learnings.

On the right of the picture, there is a trough made of wood on which small rubber balls or marbles are placed to roll from left to right down the trough. The object is to keep the balls rolling as fast as they drop into the bottom. Numbers are placed on the balls, so children roll them in order from one through ten.

In the middle are two weighing devices, on which children place weights to balance a scale. Blocks may also be used. The child is faced with the problem of getting the weights in the right position in order to balance the beam.

On the left of the picture is another device for balancing buckets of equal size. Also, on the same side, are two pulley arrangements with a ramp placed at the bottom. A block of wood, with detachable wheels,

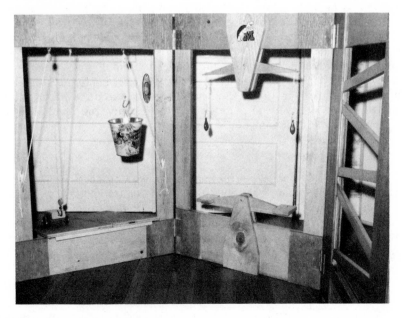

FIGURE 14–1   Interest Center

shows the child how wheels overcome friction. He discovers this by pulling the wood up the ramp without the wheels. Then the wheels are attached, to show the ease with which the wood goes up the ramp. This is a folding piece of equipment, and large enough for three or four children to use simultaneously.[1]

dominoes

Use the very large dominoes. On the blank side paste pictures of animals, flowers, etc. On other dominoes, place corresponding pictures. Have children place corresponding pictures together. This can be a matching game played by one or more children.

For the 5-year-old child numbers could be used to correspond to the number of dots on the dominoes. This gives children the concept of the number of dots that make up the number.

tossing game

Start with three or four cardboard ice cream cartons (three gallon size). Paint each container a different color or cover the cartons with contact paper.

Attach the cartons to each other by using thin wire, placing the wire on the sides of the cartons that are touching. Add a picture of flowers to each container (or pictures of animals or people). For further identification, use square pieces of various colors of paper and place on the cartons.

Children use a bean bag filled with rice (because it doesn't sting quite as much as beans) as tossing equipment. As the children toss the bags, they could tell which carton they are aiming for.

This is a game for muscular control, accuracy, identification of objects, or color identification. If the objects are placed on each carton with masking tape, the pictures may be changed from time to time to add variety to the game. The teacher may use pictures centered around the current interest of the group. She may want to introduce a trip in this manner, in which case, the pictures would be things the children would be seeing on their excursion.

design board

A large piece of acoustical tile may become a creative center by the addition of golf tees and colorful string of different lengths. The tees may be placed in the holes of the board, and children can join the tees by attaching strings in a design. Two children or more can work together—each adding one string at a time with the idea of making a design or of covering the board.

[1]Plans for this center may be purchased by writing to: Mrs. Joanne Welling, Route 2, Sykesville, Maryland 21784. © 1970 Joanne Welling.

FINGERPLAYS

An old form of dramatization or telling a short story is finger play; it is used in many school groups. To make fingerplays creative and self-expressive, the children could decide what motions or movements their fingers will make to interpret the rhyme.

In being self-expressive, children will choose movements that are comfortable for them. These will not necessarily be ones which the teacher would choose. Take this fingerplay as an example:

> Here are five soldiers standing by the door,
> One marches away and then there are four.
> Four little soldiers looking at me,
> One falls down and then there are three.
> Three little soldiers going to the zoo,
> One goes home and then there are two.
> Two little soldiers left all alone,
> One says, "Good-bye" and then there is one.
> One little soldier lifts up his gun,
> He marches away and then there are none.

For this rhyme, children might choose to bend a finger downward as each soldier leaves. They do this by using one hand to hold down the fingers of the other hand. In this way, they make the movements simpler than the adult would do them.

The child could interpret this singling out of fingers in another way. Here is another concept of five:

> Five little ducks standing in a row,
> They walk to the water, going to and fro.
> This duck cries, "Quack, quack, quack."
> This one says, "Let's go back."
> This one yells, "Stay in line."
> This one says, "The water's fine."
> The last little duck just pecked at the ground,
> Eating the bugs that crawled around.

As each duck is mentioned, the child may point to the finger by using his other hand. Pointing is easy and it enables the child to see the concept of single objects representing a larger number.

First the children should listen to the fingerplay a few times. Then the children can be asked *how* they could make five ducks stand in a row; *how* they could make the ducks walk to and fro, etc. Each child may have his own way of doing this, which should be encouraged by the teacher. Divergent thinking should be a goal for teachers to encourage.

purposes of fingerplays

Fingerplays are used for many purposes. A teacher may have one or more goals in mind, as she presents the rhymes to the children for their interpretations.

Counting. In acting out the rhymes, children often use numbers. It might be cardinal numbers, such as:

> This is one cat,
> Now two cats I see.
> Another cat will make it three.
> I add another,
> Then there are four.
> Mother cat joins them,
> To make one more.
> Now, let's count them: 1, 2, 3, 4, 5.

Here we have cardinal numbers, counting by sequence, a quantitative concept of five, and the idea of addition—all in one poem.

Counting can become more meaningful to the children if they clap the numbers as they are said:

> See the birds in the tree,
> Now let's count them: 1, 2, 3. (Clap each number)
> Now do it backwards: 3, 2, 1.
> Away fly the birds, every one.

Children could have fingerplays that include the use of ordinal numbers:

> The first little dog barked very loud.
> The second little dog ran after a crowd.
> The third little dog said, "Let's eat, let's eat!"
> The fourth little dog said, "Let's have meat!"
> The fifth little dog said, "I think I will stay,
> In my own backyard and sleep all day!"

Noise. Some fingerplays help children release noises and aggressions by using loud noises to illustrate some part of the fingerplay:

> These are my firecrackers,
> Five of them, see?
> Two are my brother's,
> And two belong to me.
> The last one's the smallest.
> It makes a small sound.

But listen to the big ones,
As I throw them on the ground.
Boom, Boom, Boom, Boom!

Home And School. Other fingerplays connect the child's home life with his school experiences:

Here is my father who works all day.
Here is my mother with whom I play.
Here is my grandfather very tall.
Here is grandmother who gave me a ball.
Here is my baby, small and sweet,
All he does is sleep and eat.

Visitors. Sometimes a play is used to emphasize the importance of an animal's visit to the school. A rabbit might cause this rhyme to be used:

My rabbit has two big ears,
And a funny little nose.
He likes to nibble carrots,
And he hops wherever he goes.

Children's Ideas. A teacher may use fingerplays to get children to suggest ideas or sounds to fit into the rhyme:

I have a space ship that makes funny sounds.
When I travel to the moon it says _____
As I fly around.

Rhyming Words. Plays give children an opportunity to select words that rhyme with other words. It is best if the rhyming lines follow each other:

See my fingers shake and shake,
See them as they make a _____.
Watch my fingers bend over so,
Until I get them very _____.
Up they stand, so very tall,
They run away and there's none left at _____.

Size And Shape. Teachers often present sizes and shapes—small, large, smaller, larger, smallest, largest, round, flat, etc.—through the use of a fingerplay:

My fingers make a circle,
One that's very small.
Now I make a big one,

Just like a rubber ball.
This is my ring finger,
This one is the smallest.
I put all my fingers together,
To see which is the tallest.

Holiday Rhymes. When holidays are celebrated, it is fun to have a fingerplay that tells about the special occasion:

Five little Valentines ready to mail,
This one's for Tommy; this one's for Dale.
This one is yellow; this one is blue.
The last one is special, it is for you.

Birthdays. Sometimes a birthday celebration can involve fingerplay. Instead of singing "Happy Birthday" to the child, a rhyme might be acted:

This is _____.
It's his birthday today.
He's _____ years old, so they say.
Let's count his age as we clap our hands,
To let him know we think he's grand.
1, 2, 3, 4, 5.

Left And Right Concept. When doing a fingerplay involving left and right motions, the teacher must be sure to stand with her back to the children, while she uses her hands. This is necessary if the preschoolers are to follow the teacher's motions, and learn directions from them. If she does the motions the correct way but stands facing the group, the children are learning the incorrect directions. Therefore, she must be sure she is moving to *the children's* right and left.

Your hand on your shoulder,
And then on your toes.
Your right hand on your knee,
Then on your lap it goes.
Place the left hand on your nose.
Touch your left hand to the floor.
Clap your hands 1, 2, 3,
Would you like to do that some more?

Dramatization. Fingerplays may be used as flannel board stories. They also may be dramatized by the children using their whole bodies instead of just their hands:

Five little kittens sitting on the floor,
One ran away and then there were four.

Four little kittens playing round a tree,
One went to sleep and then there were three.
Three little kittens beginning to "Mew,"
One climbed the tree and then there were two.
Two little kittens playing in the sun,
One went home and then there was one.
One little kitten left all alone,
He chased a mouse and then there was none.

SUMMARY

Games mean fun to any age. Young children are no exception. They enjoy the variations that may occur in selecting games; they also like the role playing and the relaxation a game affords. Through this facet of the program children are introduced to further social living, an understanding of their own and other's capabilities, conceptual learnings, language, and fair play.

Any game should include the entire group, if possible. If it is a matter of having too many children for each to have a turn, try the game in two groups at a time. Once the children learn the game, they can conduct it without a teacher's presence.

One thing to remember is that children of this age have difficulty making circles and maintaining them—holding hands helps. It is also good to continue holding hands if the children are playing a game where someone is tagged and has to chase the tagger. If hands are held, the chased child can be guided back to the *vacant* space by watching for the opening. Otherwise, he may go into any vacant space if all hands are down at the children's sides.

Try to avoid competition. Wait until the child is older and *wants* it. When you are still under age 6, it is a difficult thing to face—you can't get there in time so you are out of the game; you drop the ball so you are penalized; you can't run fast enough so you go into the "pot."

Fingerplays should not be used just for gaining quiet or attention in a group, or just for signaling the beginning or ending of some activity. There are so many good reasons and so many learnings which can be beneficial to children, and which the teacher sees as her objectives in using these rhymes.

Select rhymes that have some arithmetical phrase, some social implications, some conceptual learnings, some noisy sounds, or some sequence of events. Bring out these learnings through action of the hands, concentrating some on rhyme and rhythm. If the teacher does these with expression and enjoyment, children get a glimpse of the value of reading with expression and the variations the voice can use in speaking and changing characters.

15   the young child

his playground

The out-of-doors offers many things to the young child that cannot be found in the classroom. For one thing, the child has a larger stretch of space—one not confined by walls and ceiling—in which he may run, play, jump, and be as active as he wishes.

The school yard is also a place where noise is not restricted as it is indoors. Children may scream, speak loudly, make sounds with articles and toys, toss balls, and do all the big physical activities that are prohibited in the classroom.

Outdoor play constitutes about one-third of the preschool day. Because children are such active individuals, the playground needs equipment to supply their needs for all kinds of physical expression.

Buying playground equipment is expensive, and often not as desirable as something which could be made inexpensively by the teacher or school. This "homemade" equipment could serve more than one physical purpose, which might not be true of purchased equipment. Here is a look at some substitutes that the teacher could build, or have built, at little or no cost.

CLIMBING EQUIPMENT

The following substitutes might be made for the jungle gym, which is a wonderful climbing piece of outdoor play material.

tree gym

Using a number of tree trunks, pile the wood in a pyramid shape, and make the form secure by cementing the trunks together. The best trunks to use are those with the bark still on them, or tree trunks which have been weathered for some time. This allows for sure-footedness when children place their feet on the rough bark, which prevents sliding or slipping.

A good wood sealer purchased at a paint store may keep the bark from peeling from the tree trunks. Children can use this improvised jungle gym for climbing over, climbing along, jumping off of, and hiding behind.

reel gym

Some electric or gas companies will donate empty cable reels, which are not returnable to the manufacturer. These make a different kind of jungle gym.

The reels are bolted together to form a tower, usually consisting of about three large reels. A rope may be hung from the top to permit children to slide down, instead of climb down. A ladder with hooks at the top may be added for the more adventuresome children.

hanging rope

A large, heavy rope can be hung from a tree branch or from an L-shaped form. Knots can be tied in this rope, about every foot, to give children secure footrests for climbing.

This rope can also be used for swinging from side to side, twisting around, wrapping around the pole or tree, or holding on to when pushing away from the pole or tree.

net gym

An old commando net, or any other net made with large holes, placed in a framework or hung from a beam can become a climbing place for children. It also gives them a solid footing, which a slippery pipe or the commercial jungle gym might not offer.

ladder gym

Three discarded wooden ladders will make a jungle gym. Place two of these ladders in an upright position, and place the third ladder across the top of the other two. Cement the two upright ladders in the ground, and bolt the top ladder to the others.

If only two ladders are available, use two pieces of heavy lumber in place of the third horizontal ladder. Another way these two ladders may be used is by placing them with the tops together, to form an inverted V-shape. Whatever the shape, be sure the ladders are not too high for the children.

climbing stick

Cement a two by four into the ground after sanding it and painting it with water resistant solution. Place the board so that it stands as high as a child's head. Across this board nail or screw sturdy boards (about a foot long), not too far apart, to serve as rungs.

The result is a climbing ladder. It may even become a fireman's ladder if the teacher places a rubber hose near the stick. Activity is often suggested by an extra piece of material.

step gym

When a house is being demolished or repaired, it is possible to purchase or be given a flight of steps. About four treads are all that are needed for a climbing apparatus.

These steps are cemented into the ground, and rubber treads nailed to each step. Place a quantity of sand in the back of the steps to serve as a landing place.

Children can climb the short flight, then jump into the sand on the other side. A cleated board might also be placed near the steps, or hooked on the back of the steps. The children can then climb the steps and slide to the ground.

SANDPILE

Whether outdoors or indoors, a sandpile is a sensory experience that most children enjoy. These boxes bring about some socialization, some sharing of ideas, some quiet activity, and usually much language. Whatever types of sandpiles are used, a cover is necessary to keep the sand clean.

pool sandpile

It is always easy to find a child's bathing pool that someone is throwing away because of a leak. This discarded object can become a sandpile. It will save the cost of buying lumber to build one. The sand will act as an anchor for the pool, or the pool can be set in concrete.

bathtub sandpile

A low, discarded bathtub may be sunk into the ground and used as a sandpile. Rubber tubing may be placed around the edges of the tub for safety.

log sandpile

Four large tree trunks may be cemented in the ground. These form the rim of a sandpile. The trunks also serve as seats for children as they play in the sand.

tire sandpile

Truck tires or airplane tires make nice comfortable seats, as well as sand holders. Cement them to the ground before adding sand.

SLIDES

A child enjoys the feeling of sailing through space that he experiences as he goes down a slide. Slides for the young child should not be as high as for elementary school children. They should be sturdy and slippery enough to let him slide freely without sticking to the slide.

rope slides

Cover a heavy rope with an old plastic garden hose by threading the rope through the hose. The hose protects the children's hands as they hold the rope and slide down it. It also gives children a firmer hold when climbing up the rope.

Hang this rope from a tree, and anchor the other end to the ground. Children can climb up by using their hands and feet. Sliding down is accomplished by hanging in the air and using the hands to slide. The children may also wrap their feet around the rope and slide down by using their hands and legs.

breadboard slides

Wooden breadboards make good slides if the school has a hill nearby. These boards may also be used as sleds when snow is on the hill. Attaching ropes to the boards makes them easy to pull across the snow. Plastic trays may also be used in the same way.

wooden horse slides

A carpenter's wooden horse is a good base for holding a wide board. This board is cleated so it may be attached to the horse and become a slide.

This same piece of equipment can be used for a seesaw by placing cleats in the middle of the board so it will fit over the top of the horse.

SWINGS

Children love to swing, and again they are overcoming space. They feel a part of the air above the ground as their feet and bodies leave the solid earth, and they become master of the moving swing.

Metal and wooden swings can be dangerous if no protection is offered the children in the way of a fence, or some other barrier, to protect others who are walking in the vicinity of the moving swings. Materials that do not hurt when a child gets bumped, as he jumps out of the swing or as he leaves the swing, are best to be used with these young children.

ring swing

If a gymnasium is throwing away a hanging exercise ring, use it for a playground swing. Add suspending ropes, and the ring becomes a seat on which children can sit with legs through the ring and hands holding the rope.

rope swing

These are made by using a rope, and then adding a broom handle for use as a seat (the handle is about a foot and a half long). This is hung by tying the ropes to either side of the handle. It may also have the rope covered with rubber tubing to prevent wet fingers from freezing to the rope in cold weather.

tire swing

A large tire hanging by four ropes makes a twisting, jumping, and swinging piece of equipment for young children. A large tire permits more than one child to use the swing at the same time.

OUTDOOR PLAY HOUSE

table house

If a table is no longer useable indoors, cement the legs into the ground outdoors. Over the table, nail a piece of tarpaulin to form the sides of a house. Leave an opening on one side for easy entrance.

tent

Play houses are great fun for hiding in, or for privacy. If this kind of equipment is too costly, children can use improvised tents. These are made by placing canvas or tarpaulin over a center pole, and tying the ends to stakes in the ground.

box house

An extra large wooden box can become a house, if one side of the box is taken off. This open side will be an entrance to the house.

log cabin

A high school workshop will usually make a log house right on the school playground. Boy scouts working on certain badges will also perform this task.

Give either group the specifications, supply the small tree trunks, and the workers will do the rest. The nursery school and kindergarten children may enjoy helping to build the structure.

OTHER EQUIPMENT

There are other kinds of out-of-door equipment which may add to the activity and dramatic play of a preschool playground.

boats

A rowboat (which is no longer waterproof) can become an addition to the playground and foster dramatic play. If the oars are left in the boat, wire them securely to the oarlocks so they cannot be removed by the children.

automobiles

The chassis of an old car can often be found in a junk yard. By removing any dangerous things on the panel, and by removing tires, it becomes a part of the playground equipment.

If a smaller and cheaper automobile is desired, then the teacher may construct one of her own or have one made. Cover the outside of a wooden box (such as that used for milk delivery) with spackle. Rub it in well as a filler for the porous wood. Attach ball bearing casters to the bottom of the box.

Varnish the box, or use a nontoxic paint. Attach a three-eighths inch dowel stick to hold a small wheel—the driving wheel of the car. A small board may be placed on the inside to serve as a seat for the driver.

This toy may be used indoors or outdoors. It is a cooperative toy that needs someone to pull, push, and become a rider.

school bus

Small school buses may also be a part of the playground. The wheels are removed and any dangerous parts on the dashboard are also removed. Remove the door, also, so children will not lock themselves inside the bus.

ADDITIONS TO EXISTING PLAYGROUND EQUIPMENT

If the playground is already set up, some additions might challenge children to greater achievement. Also, the children may have "conquered" the existing equipment, and new gadgets added to old equipment may create new interest and new ideas.

slide

Add a heavy rope, knotted every foot, to the slide entrance. Children who can climb the steps of the slide in a skillful manner, may accept the challenge of a new approach to the top of the slide.

jungle gym

Place a large heavy board (five feet by ten feet) against the bars of the jungle gym. Children may walk up this ramp instead of climbing on the bars. Narrow pieces of wood—placed about six inches apart on the middle part of the board—will help some children who cannot cling to the smooth board. A rubber mat could also be used for easier ascent and descent.

sandpile

Replace the present sandpile supplies with pans and utensils used by restaurants and hotels. These may be purchased from a surplus store—large sieves, large wooden spoons, large colanders, large baking pans. Handling these objects requires greater muscular control. It often fosters socialization because help may be needed to move things or to fill them.

wheeled toys

Once the children have become proficient in manipulating bicycles and wagons, try drawing heavy white chalk lines on the floor for children to use as roads. This activity requires more eye coordination and greater muscular skill.

A regular track can be made outside by placing six-inch boards on a piece of plywood to form tracks. The boards need to be thin, so the track will not be too high, for easy manipulation of the tricycle over the track. Train signals or road signs may be added for dramatic play. Probably the children would like to make these signs.

dramatic play

Obtain a large packing box, as high as possible. Knock out both small ends, and the box becomes a tunnel through which children may ride wheeled toys.

A ramp can be added at either end for smoother entrance and exit. This box also becomes a hiding place for those who like to be alone at times.

SUMMARY

Playground equipment does not have to be the most expensive part of the school budget. Sturdy substitutes will offer the children the same physical and social stimulation. Often the homemade equipment may offer more than a bought piece of equipment, because the teacher may add little extras here and there. This is to ensure that the slide, jungle gym, and swing do not become routine and can offer further challenge when conquered.

The playground is a good spot to offer a place for real "messing" material. A mud puddle, water play, and sand may be used with more freedom outdoors than would be possible indoors.

With the child's urge to be recognized as big and strong, he has an opportunity to display his ability when he plays outside. He is more confident of his strength when one hears him say, "I can hold on now, see?" "I can do it," he glows. "Look at me," he shouts. He is learning to conquer the equipment, and his pride is evident by the triumph on his face, the happiness in his voice. The teacher watches. Once the child has accomplished a difficult task—and the challenge of the equipment has been met, she adds greater challenge to a part of the equipment to meet the growing needs of the child.

16   the young child

his creative setting

In the preceding chapters there has been an attempt to point out that creative teaching involves not only the child, but the teacher as well. The child is born with creativity which the teacher fosters by understanding the child and offering him stimulating materials to encourage him to express his own ideas and thinking. She does this through all kinds of materials and activities, some of which have been discussed in this book. The creative approach needs the proper setting in which to grow. The following ideas contribute to such an atmosphere.

PROPERTY OF CREATOR

A wonderful thing about the creativity of the very young, whether it is painting, drawing, building, modeling, talking, or playing, is that it springs from the child's imagination, his feelings, and his experiences. It is creativity in its native form. Therefore, the creating of language, art products, play, or stories is something personal. It is the child's creation. It is his own thinking, planning, and organizing, and should not be criticized or evaluated by the teacher—only encouraged.

TEACHER INTERFERENCE

If creativity is indeed a personal thing, then why do adults require specifics from children? Once the adult asks for special details, the picture, structure, story, or dramatization is no longer the child's creation. It is now a cooperative endeavor on the part of the child and teacher. It contains what both see, feel, and have experienced. It reflects the philosophy of the teacher—that only *she* knows how to think out problems and do things—and, therefore, the child must be molded to her way of creating.

TIME FOR THE CREATOR

Teachers who set a clock that requires all creative activity to stop, no matter what its stage, are really saying that creativity can be controlled by limiting the period of time. They are saying that all things should be completed when the teacher feels sufficient time has elapsed. These teachers should place themselves in the situation of the children, who must stop doing an interesting thing because the clock says so. Then it is possible that the teachers would understand the reluctance of children to stop in the exciting part of a production, conversation, or play to change to something else.

VARIATIONS IN MATERIALS

Children should be offered a variety of materials from which to choose each day, and not every child should be doing the same thing. There may be special times when everyone makes cookies, everyone helps trim the Christmas tree, everyone dyes Easter eggs—but even then the materials offer a selection of choices. In this manner, the teacher caters to individual differences and realizes that everyone has times when certain materials appeal to him more than others. She also realizes that children's appetites for playing and working can be satisfied through a selection from different types of materials—some more mature than others.

WORKING CONDITIONS

A teacher should always be aware of the working conditions her room affords. Is there enough space on the floor for building and playing? Is the table large enough to make working there comfortable, and does it offer enough space for large objects? Is the light coming in the windows directly in the eyes of the children, or directly on the paper or the book they are using? If so, what is happening to the children's play, work, and especially their eyes?

SOMETHING OLD, SOMETHING NEW

The nursery school and kindergarten can strengthen old learnings and, at the same time, introduce new ones based on the learnings of the past. So, many schools place "cute" pictures of dogs and cats around the walls, usually a portrait kind of picture. This might be a known learning. In order to take it a step further and bring in the unknown, the teacher could find pictures of police dogs in action, seeing-eye dogs at work, rescue dogs helping someone, or performing dogs in a circus. In this way, children could learn more about the many roles that dogs play in this world.

ALONE OR TOGETHER

Does the material of the schoolroom offer children opportunities to play in groups, and also opportunity to play alone? There are some days when children would rather be by themselves, and work on things without the association of others. There are times when groups of children need to work together, and must have enough supplies to carry on cooperative play. Creativity may be a one-man activity, or may be group sponsored.

SUMMARY

A teacher who wishes to aid the young child in becoming an effective member of his society will need to utilize the good educational resources of the past. She will also take present day resources which are profitable, and project the developments of the future, as she sees them, which might affect the child in his life.

So, the teacher endeavors to make the nursery school and kindergarten a place where:

1. Materials lead to problem solving and thinking.
2. Patience, skill, interest, and delight are fostered.
3. Trips, talking, and listening add to intellectual background.
4. Creating, in all facets of the program, is a daily occurrence.
5. Adults and children talk and listen.
6. Children talk and listen to other children.
7. Materials are presented in sequence.
8. Concepts are learned.
9. Words are clarified.
10. Children discover spatial concepts.

11. Children make predictions about what will happen.
12. Children discuss and discover what is in pictures.
13. Children watch as the teacher writes their names.
14. Teachers and children handle books properly.
15. Children learn that books are a resource for information.
16. Children grow in use of large and small muscles.
17. Children learn about themselves and others.
18. Teachers give children an exciting, stimulating, and appropriate program based on objectives.
19. Teachers maintain an inquisitiveness about things, and foster this same inquisitiveness in children.
20. Above all other things, children and teachers discover it is pleasurable to be learning in a group situation.